MAKING A LIFE

IS MAKING WAVES!

"This book will motivate you to reach for your dreams and grab them."

—Candice Carpenter, chairman of the board, iVillage.com

"If your career has lost its meaning, this book will give you the courage to start over. That's a great gift."

—John Naisbitt, author of *Megatrends*

"Highly evocative. . . . There's a revolution in values sweeping through American business, and Mark Albion has his finger on its pulse."

—Norman Lear, television writer/producer and founder, The Business Enterprise Trust

For more information, please contact:
www.makingalife.com

MAKING A LIFE, MAKING A LIVING®

RECLAIMING YOUR PURPOSE ——— AND PASSION ——— IN BUSINESS AND IN LIFE

MARK ALBION

WARNER
BUSINESS
BOOKS™

Published by Warner Books

A Time Warner Company

Warner Business Books are published by Warner Books, Inc., 1271 Avenue of the Americas, New York, NY 10020

Visit our Web site at www.twbookmark.com

A Time Warner Company

The Warner Business Book logo is a trademark of Warner Books, Inc.

Making a Life, Making a Living is a registered trademark of Mark Albion

Originally published in hardcover by Warner Books

First Trade Printing: December 2000

10 9 8 7 6 5 4 3 2 1

The Library of Congress has cataloged the hardcover edition as follows:
Albion, Mark S.
    Making a life, making a living : reclaiming your purpose and passion in business and in life / Mark Albion.
        p.   cm.
        Includes index.
        ISBN 0-446-52404-2
        1. Industrial management—Vocational guidance. 2. Executives.
    3. Career development. 4. Career changes. 5. Self-actualization (Psychology)
    I. Title.
    HD38.2.A347   2000
    658.4'09—dc21   99-30166
                                                     CIP

    ISBN 0-446-67651-9 (pbk.)

Book design by Giorgetta Bell McRee
Cover design by Michael Accordino

To Amanda,
who has taught me
about compassion for others,

and

Nicolette,
who has taught me
about passion and enthusiasm.

ACKNOWLEDGMENTS

**The world is full of willing people,
some willing to work, the rest willing to let them.**
—ROBERT FROST

For my twenty-first birthday, family friends took me to Switzerland on a ski vacation. It was my first trip to Europe, and I was not disappointed.

The skiing was great. One sun-drenched day, older "brother" Paul and I skied into Italy. A local bus picked us up to take us back to the lifts so we could return to Switzerland. The bus never made it.

The driver stopped the bus in the middle of the road, got out, and sat down outside a tavern for a drink of wine. We were told that he felt "it is too beautiful a day to drive a bus. It is a day to enjoy the sun and the air, the sky and the mountains, the life all around us."

The passengers got off the bus, rocked it from side to side, and tipped it over, leaving it in the middle of the street. Paul and I got our skis and walked the several miles back to the lift. It was a wonderful hike, a special day—time we would never have shared if not for that bus driver's "crazy" priorities.

That day I was told of an old Italian expression: "Once the game is over, the king and the pawn go back into the same box." It's an expression I have never forgotten.

I would like to acknowledge that bus driver. His attitude toward life as an expression of joyous love is one we can easily lose sight of in our busyness. His inspiration led me to backpack around the world the next year and try to write my first book. It only took another twenty-seven years for that book to be published!

I am interested in why the apple falls.
The company wants me to catch it and make applesauce.
—H. J. SHAW

Helen Rees gave me the opportunity to do this book. She talked with Larry Kirshbaum, president of Warner Books, who was willing to give us an advance without one word written. He then brought us executive editor Rick Wolff, who instantly understood what this book was about. He has been a true compass for me when I lose my way.

Helen then introduced me to Donna Carpenter, chief executive officer of Wordworks, Inc. Donna brought in Martha Lawler to manage the project and Maurice Coyle to help structure my thinking. It was a mysterious process for this novice, but Donna made sense out of my ramblings, put poetry into my phrases. James Joyce's wife once challenged him, "Why don't you write books people can read?" Clearly he didn't have Donna Carpenter.

This book would not have been possible without the chapter subjects—my personal heroes. They opened their private lives to help us learn more about ourselves.

In particular, Judy George and Mike Barr have personally mentored me through this stage of my "middlessence." They continue to dedicate their energy to my success. Elliot Hoffman has made me face life's biggest questions. Nick Gleason represents what our young, best, and brightest can do. And what can I say about Leni Joyce, my mother? It's wonderful to be forty-eight years old and still have someone who truly worries about you every day.

If men can run the world, why can't they stop wearing neckties? How intelligent is it to start the day by tying a little noose around your neck?
—LINDA ELLERBEE

All of this work really began with my introduction in 1989 to the Social Venture Network (SVN) by Geralyn White-Dreyfous. That organization and its spin-offs today span the globe. They exist in large part because of the efforts of Josh Mailman.

Josh has given his time and resources to create and sustain these organizations at critical times. I believe he has done as much as anyone of my generation to promote socially responsible business around the world.

Others in SVN have inspired me. Most notable is my good friend Jerry Gordé, who has challenged every belief I have felt sure of and usually argued me into the ground. Bob Dunn has displayed the energy that ultimately led to developing one of our most successful organizations, Businesses for Social Responsibility. And Doris Cadoux, Arno and Evelyn Jaffe, Walter Link, and Rena Shulsky have been special friends in times of doubt and need.

One of SVN's offspring, Students for Responsible Business (SRB), connected me with young people who reignited my passion for business and service. In particular, Ron Gerrans has supported me in many ways, first as an MBA candidate at Wharton, today as an adviser on the world of his generation. I am glad to see my good friend Peter Patch now involved with SRB.

My grandfather's a little forgetful, but he likes to give me advice. One day, he took me aside and left me there.
—RON RICHARDS

ACKNOWLEDGMENTS

Grandparents Nathan and Anne Cohen taught me about values and community responsibility. Most important, they taught me about love and how it feels to be completely loved.

My wife, Joy, is her namesake for those lucky enough to know her. For over twenty years she has allowed me the space and given the support I need to be, as my father once said of my nature, "predictably unpredictable."

It is true that the observation "Your manuscript is both good and original, but the parts that are good are not original, and the parts that are original are not good" came from Samuel Johnson. But it could have come from my close and trusted friend Deb Imershein.

Deb began this journey with me in 1997 (or did it start in college in 1972?), with unexpected results. We went our separate ways after a year—for the better, as we each needed to find our own path. She continues to be my guiding light, a mirror for my soul, and a blessing to all she touches.

Two Brazilian women of petite size but powerful carriage have had an impact without knowing. Eva Passos, who helps maintain the livability of our home, told me during one of my days of despair, "Don't worry. This will all work out. You do good things for people. It will come back to you."

Cousin Sara Klabin has connected me to a branch of my family I learned of only in my twenties and to a legacy that reaffirms my values and beliefs.

> **Life may have no meaning. Or, even worse,**
> **it may have a meaning of which I disapprove.**
> —ASHLEIGH BRILLIANT

As I mention in chapter 3, I feel particularly blessed to have met Rabbi Henry and Barbara Zoob. They have created an inclusive community at Temple Beth David that has brought new meaning and joy into my family's life. The members of our Saturday morning Bible study group have inspired much of my writing the past four years.

Each Saturday my friends and I question the lessons of the teachings, accepting nothing at face value. Jon Stewart said it well: "Thou shall not kill. Thou shall not commit adultery. Don't eat pork. I'm sorry, what was that last one? Don't eat pork. God has spoken. Is that the word of God, or is that the pigs trying to outsmart everybody?"

On one thing we do agree: God's grace is everywhere. I have often thought that if I'd been born in another country or another time, I might still be a business school professor—not allowed to leave something I was pretty good at to try to find my way. I am thankful for that divine opportunity.

> **Our kids are God's message to us . . . God's way of delivering the future in the present. Our kids deliver what life sometimes only promises to deliver.**
> —NOAH BEN SHEA

Finally, I am most thankful for the gift of children.

As with most endeavors, this book took more time than I expected. That meant that when Nikki and Amanda really wanted me to get off my "[com]puter" and play with them, I often couldn't. That's why when Nikki is asked what her father does for a living, she answers simply, "He types."

I hope they'll understand. They inspire me and, at times, tire me. But I can't imagine life without them and their unique brand of wisdom that cuts right to the heart. To conclude with the words of Mark Twain: "What makes kids so smart? They tell you what they know and then they stop."

CONTENTS

You make a living by what you get.
You make a life by what you give.
—WINSTON CHURCHILL

PART 1

✳

WHO ARE YOU?

Find Your Passion

CHAPTER 1

✳

MAKE HAPPINESS
A HABIT

A Personal Odyssey

---

*Every person I have known who has been truly happy,
has learned how to serve others.*

—ALBERT SCHWEITZER

> **The trouble with the rat race is that even if you win,**
> **you're still a rat.**
> —LILY TOMLIN

The rainy morning of June 5, 1986, was the high point of my thirty-five-year-old life—or so it seemed at the time. I was full of anticipation, and no downpour could dampen my spirits. That afternoon I was scheduled to pick up a gleaming new black Jaguar, my first drop-dead trophy purchase. It said, "Okay, world, look at me. On top! In heaven!"

I had it made—Mark Albion, little big man, wunderkind professor at Harvard Business School, hotshot consultant getting richer by the minute, and still younger than some of my students! I was so full of myself then that I had best use the third person in describing the Mark Albion of 1986.

At Harvard, Mark Albion taught his own second-year course in retailing. All first-year students watched his instructional videos and pored over his case studies. Nationally recognized as one of America's top young business professors, he was profiled on CBS's *60 Minutes*. The dean of the business school warmly noted his growing celebrity in an official memo to all faculty.

Mark was making money beyond his wildest dreams. His visibility allowed him to charge a consulting fee of $5,000 a day, and he thought nothing of directing the Coca-Cola Company to send a limousine to his Boston office and chauffeur him directly to meetings in New York.

He was also co-owner of a nutritional-supplement company that raked in $60 million in its first six months. With his compensation rate at 1 percent of sales, a single month's check was enough to buy two Jaguars, not just one.

Mark was on the short list with one other candidate to become the nutritional company's next chief executive officer. If that happened—and all signs looked good—he had just about decided to quit Harvard and get really rich. He was also being courted by the Reagan administration for a subcabinet post.

In any event, Mark was seriously thinking of selling his fancy house in suburban Wellesley Hills, Massachusetts, and buying something even higher on the food chain, maybe in some gated enclave you could not even drive into in anything less than a Jag.

Then the phone rang. It was Mark Albion's wake-up call from hell.

Life is like a coin. You can spend it any way you wish,
but you can only spend it once.
—MIGUEL DE CERVANTES

We all have crises in our lives. The question is, How do we handle them? How do they affect us? This one changed my life.

My mother was on the phone: "I'd like to see you this afternoon. I have something we need to talk about."

My heart sank. Mom was back in town, having come home early from a Chicago business trip. And she was virtually demanding to see me—not at all like her.

I had never known my mother to unexpectedly cut short a business trip. Nor does she ever demand to see me. We see each other weekly, talk almost daily. Demands are unnecessary. Something was wrong with my mom.

We set a time of 4:30 P.M., right after my wife, Joy, and I picked up the new Jag.

My mood now matched the weather. The London-like fog clouded my brain. In the pouring rain, Joy and I drove to the dealership.

Our salesperson gave us a tour of the car, showing us how everything worked. But there I was, sitting atop the mountain, Mr. Success himself, and all I could do was stare at the windshield wipers and the pelting rain. I thought of the opening line of *A Tale of Two Cities:* "It was the best of times, it was the worst of times . . ." I sensed the worst.

We finished the run-through and drove the Jag home. Right at 4:30, Mom appeared. I can still see her sitting herself down—uncomfortably—on our custom-made, leather living room couch from Denmark. "I have something to tell you," she began. "I have cancer."

As Mom said, "Cancer concentrates"—just the way Samuel Johnson once described a cancer of his time: "When a man knows he is to be hanged . . . it concentrates his mind wonderfully."

She needed an operation immediately, followed by several months of chemotherapy, then a final checkup operation.

I called her doctor. He told me the truth he felt unable to tell her: "Mark, your mother's cancer is very advanced, stage four. It has moved through her entire system into her liver. We are going to do what we can. We hope she will live another six months. Unfortunately, I can't promise you more than that, and that is only fifty-fifty."

You can imagine my first reaction: "What? Let's try that again."

It didn't work. After that, I got very busy thinking about what to do next. Should I tell her? I preferred honesty, but it wasn't that simple. Spirit is so important in fighting disease. I decided not to tell her the full diagnosis.

The only issue was whether or not to operate. That was not a tough decision for me. If there was the least chance, I wanted her to have it. Don't hesitate, I told the surgeon. She's only fifty-eight—and she's my mom.

**A tragic irony of life is that we so often
achieve success . . . after the reason
for which we sought it has passed.**
—Ellen Glasgow

During the ensuing months, Joy and I visited my mother almost daily. Lots of time to reflect. Lots of time . . . except I always thought my mother and I would have so much more time together.

Waves of questions overwhelmed me: What is going on? Why can't I fix this—throw some money at it and make it all better? When will this nightmare go away?

I was angry—not just at the passage of time, but especially at myself. Why was I doing what I was doing? What price glory? Why run so fast if I had no mother around to be proud of me?

During those months of not knowing, I came to cherish a relationship that before had never been as close as pretended. And I learned a lot. I learned that my mother dragged herself into her office, lying on the floor next to her desk because she could not sit at it. She was there because she loved her work so much. Would I do that?

My mother was still alive the next March when the doctors opened her up again to operate. I was told that if they found anything they could not take care of easily, they would just close her up and let her live the rest of her precious few days in peace, maybe all the way until summer.

I was numb—afraid to feel anything real, I guess. I waited for the call.

The phone rang. The doctors had taken a look and decided not to operate further. I swallowed hard. There was a pause, and then the doctor used a beautiful five-letter word: *"Clean,"* he said, "your mother is clean." No sign of any cancer—complete microscopic absence.

The doctors were ecstatic. I was stunned. Days passed before I could grasp the miracle: Mom had been given a second life. And in the process, Mark Albion had been given a second life, too. What would we do with these gifts?

Give of your hands to serve and your hearts to love.
—MOTHER TERESA

Mom had made it with the help of love, luck, and a never-say-die attitude. She threw herself into work with even more passion and energy. During the next decade she took dramatic business risks, created new products, and built a company nationally praised for its unique market niche, humanistic working conditions, and community efforts.

A touch of grace came that September: her first grandchild, Amanda, was born and would fulfill Mom's personal dream of becoming a ballerina. Mom had always wanted a little girl in addition to a son. If cancer had won, she never would have met her beloved Amanda.

Mom was blessed with another special grandchild in 1991, Nicolette. She is a devoted grandmother, a CEO who makes sure she spends ample time with her grandchildren at least once a week. She has shown me—and hundreds of others—that one courageous person can indeed make a difference. Her full story concludes this book.

That crisis helped me build a special relationship with my mother, one that might have been impossible without the catalyst of cancer. But the question remained: Would I have the courage to follow my own path now that I had been jolted into understanding?

There is only one success—
to spend your life in your own way.
—CHRISTOPHER MORLEY

8

When you spend most of your life pursuing the material rewards that the culture encourages you to pursue, it is not easy to obey some inner voice and suddenly say, "Stop! Enough! I want to exit the fast track and live the life I should live while there is still time."

No, it is not easy to give yourself permission to change gears and combine making a life with making a living. We are not supported to do so, either. For most hardworking businesspeople, the whole idea sounds farfetched.

"Meaningful work?" my friends teased. "Isn't that a spoiled boomer concept?"

But I suddenly felt the emptiness of what just yesterday I had called success. Having acquired all the trappings that everyone around me longed for, I discovered they were now nothing more than meaningless ornaments.

While my high-paying, high-prestige job made me the envy of neighbors, I felt the life being sucked out of me, leaving me homesick for some place I could not name. I often heard myself say, "Doing research on the use of brand names is not cancer research. How did I end up doing this?"

I had broken one of my own guidelines—Don't get really good at something you don't want to do—and I was paying the price: an inauthentic life.

What had happened to the me I used to know?

How could I integrate my need for spirituality and love with my desire for material comforts and the good life? How could I stop keeping score the old way and start keeping score a new way? How could I build a truly successful, happy life—one of significance? How could I spend my life in a community of people whom I loved and who loved me in return?

**Is there anyone so wise
as to learn by the experience of others?**
—VOLTAIRE

This book is my response to those questions as told through the lives of a tribe of people I have met on my journey over the past decade. Like the pilgrims in *The Canterbury Tales,* we are all travelers in search of the truth—a truth we would happily serve with our lives. They, too, have had their crises. They, too, have struggled with finding passion and purpose in their careers, with integrating their love for family and community with their work.

They are my heroes, my teachers. Their stories illustrate twelve important guidelines, organized under four questions, that will help you be the author of your own life story: Who are you? What do you want? What can you do? Where are you going?

The guidelines constitute a framework that many MBAs, managers, and executives I work with use to make a life while also making a living—guidelines for living a life of significance. After all, aren't we all the heroes of our own life stories?

Adults are always asking kids what they want to be when they grow up 'cause they're trying to get ideas.
—PAULA POUNDSTONE

When I speak at leading business schools, I ask students two questions: What did you dream of being and doing before you felt compelled to get an MBA? And who are your heroes?

Less than 5 percent of these talented people in their late twenties know what they really want to do. Nor have the vast majority ever known in such a way as to make them feel they could make a living doing it.

By contrast, more than seven thousand MBA students have responded to my heroes question with exemplary names heavily weighted in favor of those who served humankind: Muhammad Ali, Jimmy Carter, Dr. Martin Luther King Jr., Albert Schweitzer, Mother Teresa. Moms and dads are mentioned often. So, too, are important personal teachers. Few businesspeople make the list.

Most MBAs admire people for their hearts more than their heads—they admire people who do good. But why, if you greatly respect one way of life, would you feel compelled to pursue an entirely different course?

"We are shaped and fashioned by what we love," wrote the great German poet Goethe. So if we spend our lives doing what we don't love, we risk paying a heavy price: a disconnected soul that lacks a true home. And lives of work out of balance with who we want to become.

It isn't easy to give yourself permission to pursue your dreams, follow your heroes, and seek your inner truth. It isn't easy to work to express your true self rather than playing a role that isn't you and answering a calling that something or someone else has determined for you.

Mother Teresa said it best. "To work without love is slavery."

Work should be a vehicle for that heroism. The ancient Swedish term for business is *nårings liv*, which literally means "nourishment for life." In the Chinese language, too, there are three-thousand-year-old symbols for business that translate into "life" or "live with meaning": work as an expression of life.

Each story is a portrait of someone trying to truly have it all—by making a difference and being nourished by work. All want to fit a meaningful, financially successful career into their lives.

Each story was written to raise several questions. Each ends with a short prescription offering my personal lifelines. Read the stories alone or with family and friends. Read them most especially with your children. Read them out loud. Read them in any order you choose. Like the shortest distance between two points, the path to a better life is not always a straight line.

**Until you make peace with who you are,
you'll never be content with what you have.**
—DORIS MORTMAN

I finally did leave Harvard—not an easy choice with so many great opportunities. Although my mother's crisis pushed me to leave, I actually had known earlier that this culture was not for me. My values didn't fit the system. But it took time and a blow to the heart to give me the strength to do something about it.

It's not always easy to articulate why you aren't jumping out of bed every morning to go to work. I know why in retrospect, but at the time the reality was too muddled, too confounding.

There I was with one of the best jobs at one of the world's greatest institutions. I had brilliant colleagues, unlimited resources, few bosses, a flexible work schedule, a challenging learning environment, and no financial concerns—all in my hometown.

How could I not be happy?

The signposts were right in front of me, but I couldn't see them. I saw only what I wanted to see. I didn't want to hear what friends or family could readily have told me. I needed to seek my truth elsewhere.

So, in the summer of 1988, after spending nearly twenty years of my life in various capacities at one institution, my identity changed from Professor Mark S. Albion, Harvard Business School, to Mark Albion.

I was on my own—a soloist.

There is an expression: "No amount of travel on the wrong road will get you to the right destination." At least now I had a chance to get on the right road.

Still, it would take ten years from my mother's cancer announcement before I could finally give myself permission to try to become someone I respected. It would take the personal satisfaction of my first speech from the heart before I could allow myself to try to become that person, a person known today simply as "Dr. Mark."

The eyes of my eyes are opened.
—E. E. CUMMINGS

That decade can best be described as my "middlessence"— a term invented by the life-stage researcher Gail Sheehy, author of the significant book *Passages*. It was a period of starting another age of life, one more attuned to seeking my truth.

The first step was to stop doing what was making me unhappy. Next, I had to find a way to act on my desire for change.

My first search, not surprisingly, was within the existing structures I knew so well—the world of big business and strategy consulting.

But nothing really changed until I looked outside the traditional structures and inside myself. What did I want to do? Something that would make me happy? Yes. Something that would prove fulfilling? Yes, again. Once I allowed those thoughts to surface, I ran up against the usual fear and doubt: "Great idea, Mark, but how will you make a living?"

Soon after I left Harvard, I began to realize that chief executives who used to return my calls didn't anymore. The speech-making requests stopped, too.

I was forced to seek out a new group of people, a new type of executive. One asked me to do some strategic planning. I began the work, only to be told after two days that all the plans I had directed were "garbage." He said, "If we don't find a way, a strategy, to help our front-line service people find meaning in their jobs every day, none of this will happen."

I felt miserable. Still on automatic pilot, I didn't yet have the guts to do what that young executive so perceptively and courageously suggested: Develop a plan for meaning, for trust, for community—just like what you should design for your own life.

I got invited into a group of socially conscious entrepreneurs, the Social Venture Network, and began to meet others who held values similar to mine. In my former life as a professor, these people had been invisible to me—and I to them. Now they began to populate my world, giving me strength to grow and change. Today they are my community.

But as much as I enjoyed being a socially conscious entrepreneur in the late 1980s and early 1990s, that still wasn't it. Something was missing.

There are years that ask questions, and years that answer.
—ZORA NEALE HURSTON

In 1993 the Social Venture Network helped launch an organization for MBAs called Students for Responsible Business (SRB). My affection for SRB made me realize how much I missed teaching and writing—but this time I set out to focus on issues important to me. My mother's cancer had taught me at least that much.

I began to speak at business schools, enjoying the energy, enthusiasm, and dedication to service of many of these young people.

In January 1996 I directed a national electronic survey of MBA candidates' values. My purpose was to demonstrate that these students cared about more than just money.

Our SRB representatives volunteered to enlist students to fill out the surveys at each of the top fifty business schools. I began writing an electronic newsletter to stay in touch with and motivate our reps. We finished with more than 2,300 completed surveys.

On June 5, 1996, I got the opportunity to thank those dedicated students for the incredible job they had done. I was slotted to give a fifteen-minute speech at a United Nations conference and in that speech would be able to thank the student reps by name.

I never expected that the speech would also start me on a new path.

Be the change you wish to see in the world.
—MAHATMA GANDHI

Perfectly placed in a city that spans two continents, the Istanbul conference gave me a rare chance to meet and mingle with representatives from around the world. Many were remarkable individuals.

Take Ghanian Nat Nuno-Amarteifio, the gifted, compassionate mayor of Accra's three million people. Or Sylvana Maric, a Bosnian engineer living with children deprived of the chance to attend school for the past four years in a household limited to three liters of potable water a day.

Then there was Cornelia McDonald, a great-granddaughter of African American slaves, who found purpose in touring the United States with her one-woman play to teach courage, strength, and self-esteem to those in need.

What struck me most was that we all wanted the same things—the same good life. We were all dreaming the same dream.

I thought about our kinship as I waited to give my prepared speech. Before doing so, however, I promised myself two things. First, I would not be nervous. During my two and a half hours on the dais (there were five speeches during our session), I would just sit back, have fun, and enjoy this opportunity. Second, I would speak in my own style, my own voice.

Although I was forty-five years old, I had never done this before. Pretty sad commentary for one who had spent most of his life as an educator of some sort! But I had always gone by the book—just not my book. I didn't have the courage or the confidence to be myself, whoever that was.

Five minutes before my turn arrived, I decided to throw away my prepared text, copies of which the translators had before them in several languages. Instead, I would speak from the heart. It was Dr. Mark's first appearance. It was at least the beginning, I feel, of being on the right road, to find my truth, my happiness.

I simply spoke about things I cared about. About my children and my own daughter's reaction to a homeless man in Boston: "What are we going to do about him, Daddy? How are we going to help? Why are there homeless people?"

Surprisingly, when I spoke from the heart, other people seemed to hear me a little better. And for once, giving a speech was fun.

Scatter joy.
—RALPH WALDO EMERSON

After Istanbul, I felt energized. I didn't know where this would take me—I still don't—but I guess that's part of the mystery and the magic.

I continued my newsletter, as people told me that it provided a voice previously missing in their lives.

Readership and e-mails grew. I began to see an opportunity to write stories about some of the members of this business community as exemplars for young people. In August the first stories appeared.

The newsletter attracted some national attention; the

press began to call me "Dr. Mark, spiritual guru of the MBAs." In 1997 readership expanded to eighty-seven countries, and in 1998 businesspeople of all ages and backgrounds began to subscribe. College friend Deb Imershein and I started a for-profit career management firm to complement it, You & Company (www.you-company.com).

Our aspirations are our possibilities.
—ROBERT BROWNING

A study of business school graduates tracked the careers of 1,500 people from 1960 to 1980. From the beginning, the graduates were grouped into two categories. Category A consisted of people who said they wanted to make money first so that they could do what they really wanted to do later—after they had taken care of their financial concerns. Those in category B pursued their true interests first, sure that money eventually would follow.

What percentage fell into each category?

Of the 1,500 graduates in the survey, the money-now category A's comprised 83 percent, or 1,245 people. Category B risk takers made up 17 percent, or 255 graduates.

After twenty years there were 101 millionaires in the group. One came from category A, 100 from category B.

The study's author, Srully Blotnick, concluded that "the overwhelming majority of people who have become wealthy have become so thanks to work they found profoundly absorbing. . . . Their 'luck' arose from the accidental dedication they had to an area they enjoyed."

No heart has ever suffered
when it goes in search of its dreams.
—PAULO COEHLO

Each of the twelve guidelines in this book has come from experiences on my journey through middlessence. The guidelines are illustrated by the life stories of some of the most successful businesspeople I know. These individuals have built careers that integrate their lives with their work. All enjoy financial security. Some are very rich.

They have done it in large measure through love. After all, isn't most of what we do in life a way of gaining a bit more love?

All of my heroes have refused to drift through false lives. Like many businesspeople, they conformed too long to cultures that stifled their inner values and left them untrue to selves they barely recognized.

But instead of giving in to self-pity, each in his or her way summoned the will to act, to seize opportunity, to take charge of their lives. Each staged a *coup de vie,* a masterstroke of self-liberation. What their stories confirm, of course, is the age-old truth that every person's life is his or hers to lose.

I am capable of what every other human is capable of.
—MAYA ANGELOU

✳

Lifelines

Don't we all need to begin our journey by asking the question What do we truly value? As Deepak Chopra pointed out, "A life of purpose is the purpose of life."

Many of us do things backward. We blindly seek the jobs that will allow us to make the money and obtain the status that we think we need, and then we try to find out what is really important in our life.

Instead, you first need to express your own truth and serve it through your work. As Epictetus said nearly two thousand years ago, "Know first who you are. Then dress accordingly."

That takes reflection and action. It means throwing off the confining cloak of "should dos" and "have to dos" to find yourself by serving others—doing the things you love to do and are good at doing, doing the kinds of things your heroes do.

Though the mind knows the direction, the heart knows the path to creative love and joyful purpose.

The point of this little book is simple: Life is too short to squander. So work only at what really matters. Make a living that ensures a life of giving and loving. Entitle yourself to your world's standing ovation.

Now turn the page and begin reading about Tom Reis, the first of the remarkable people who helped me change my life. His story may do the same for you.

What we are seeking is . . . the rapture of being alive.
—JOSEPH CAMPBELL

CHAPTER 2

✳

KEEP YOUR WALKING COSTS LOW

Tom Reis's Walkabout

A man becomes a creature of his uniform.

—NAPOLEON

> **We should not let our fears hold us back
> from pursuing our hopes.**
> —JOHN FITZGERALD KENNEDY

What Tom Reis perceived as prohibitive "walking costs" in his first big corporate job were, to his wife, Anne, an illusion. They were on a vacation, visiting national parks out west, when Tom's perspective began to clear.

It was a stressful time for Tom at the Pillsbury Company. He was on the "hypo list" (fast-track promotions) and starting to make major money. But he wasn't happy.

His drinking was getting out of hand . . . too often, too much. So much that it was becoming a serious problem. He was becoming an alcoholic.

Anxieties about his life and work crowded his mind. His marriage became strained.

The problem wasn't the job per se—Tom found marketing intriguing, liked strategic planning and working with researchers. He enjoyed implementation, too.

"What I didn't like," Tom recounts, "was the whole lifestyle, the whole culture, the whole life I was beginning to lead and that I could see myself buying into. What I really hated was the prospect of doing this for the rest of my life.

"I didn't know how I was going to get out of this, and it really wasn't what I wanted to do in life. I didn't know what I wanted to do, but I knew that I didn't want to do this."

That night in the park lodge, Tom was thinking so hard about his troubles that he could not sleep. In the morning Anne asked him what was wrong.

"I'm feeling totally unbalanced," he told her. "I hate my work."

"Why don't you quit?" asked Anne.

"I can't quit."

"Why not?"

"We've got the house. We've got the cars. We've got all these *things.*"

Anne countered: "We can sell the house. I've got a job. We can keep bread on the table. You don't have to do this."

"I have to admit," Tom says, remembering the moment, "I was so out of whack that quitting had not crossed my mind. It didn't seem to be an option. Anne just helped me over that hurdle."

From then on, Tom Reis made sure to keep his walking costs low.

**I always wanted to be somebody,
but I should have been more specific.**
—Lily Tomlin

A close friend of mine has become good at a job he no longer wants to do. He recorded the second highest number of billable hours in his more than thousand-person law firm in 1996—the same year his wife gave birth to their second child.

For some fifteen years now my friend has dreamed about doing something else. But he is afraid to give up his partnership. He thinks he has too much to lose—and he can't quite grasp how much he has to gain. His wife knows, but . . .

Imagine yourself in the same state. You are a lawyer with the prestigious firm of Nails, Knives, Shredders & Fists. After years of running on the fast track, you have finally arrived.

You are a partner. You are at the apex of your profession,

at the top of your game, a star. You have all the rewards that go with that lofty status—a fantastic house, kids in private schools, a luxury car, ski trips, golf outings, Caribbean getaways.

You've invested heavily in your profession. First, there were the costs for schooling, borne in part by your parents, who have certainly been enjoying the reflected glory of having a child who's a partner at Nails, Knives.

But it's more than just money. You've invested years in getting to where you are today. You harbored expectations about the kind of life you wanted to lead, the kind of people you wanted to be with, the future you saw for yourself.

Admittedly, along the way you've done some things of which you aren't particularly proud. You kept silent when you knew you should have spoken up. You turned a blind eye when it hurt to pretend you had not seen what you did see. Yes, you paid your dues for success.

There's only one problem. You *hate* your job. You wake up every morning dreading work. The success you've achieved doesn't seem worth it.

> **Fear not that thy life shall come to an end,**
> **but rather fear that it shall never have a beginning.**
> —JOHN CARDINAL NEWMAN

As you adjust your well-tailored suit before the mirror each day, you are really looking past the image to days, months, years of dissatisfaction stretching before you. It's not a pretty reflection. You say you're going to change, but . . .

You feel trapped. You feel the costs of walking away are too high. Who would pay the mortgage and the tuition bills and the club dues? Every time you think you have some breathing room, it seems that another unexpected bill drops on your desk.

What's more, you don't know how to do anything else. You went from undergraduate school to law school, from law school to Nails, Knives. If you had to do something else in life, you think you would probably fail.

Besides, this is who you are. This is what everyone expects you to be—a high-priced lawyer in a high-powered firm. The role you play is what your spouse bargained for, the parent your children recognize. It's how you are introduced at social functions, how you are seen in your community. It's also how you think of yourself.

You could never walk away from it. Or could you?

Now, change "lawyer" to corporate manager, investment banker, journalist, software consultant, or fund manager. Change "partner" to vice president, director, executive committee member, senior editor, or division head. Change the fictitious Nails, Knives, Shredders & Fists to the name of your organization.

Do you love your job? Do you wake up every morning eager to get to work? If not, could you walk away from it? Can you afford to?

Yes, you can.

We do not remember days; we remember moments.
—CESARE PARESO

After college I backpacked around the world, working as I went, with no plans, no goals. Near the end of that trip I had a moment that I often return to, a moment of freedom. It helps me think of the rewards of a life lived.

I was twenty-three, going somewhere in the back of a pickup truck. After a night of camping out on a South Pacific island, here I was, the warm morning sun on my face, the wind blowing in my hair—just me, my backpack, a pickup truck. Nothing else in the world. I was *free to be.* I will never

25

forget that all-encompassing, blissful feeling. Nor would I trade it for most anything.

To get to that moment was not easy. It, too, had what I call "walking costs"—heavy baggage filled with money, expectations, and personal identification was left behind.

The fact is, once you get used to a way of living, of doing things, it can be hard to walk away, hard to switch. There is little outside support and certainly no constituency for change.

I graduated from a good college and was the only one of seven roommates who did not go directly to law school, business school, or both.

What was my problem? "How will this look on his résumé?" wondered the parents of my friends. Most of them would look at me with a jaundiced eye until I returned to graduate school two years later.

Not surprisingly, the more experience you have walking, the easier it gets. The perceived costs, however, may get higher. Money is part of it, but often the least of it. The most painful is the loss of self-esteem and standing in other people's eyes.

But, as a good deal of research has shown, the patterns for decision making that we set in our twenties and early thirties are hard to change later.

> **The trouble with life in the fast lane is that**
> **you get to the other end in an awful hurry.**
> —JOHN JENSEN

Over the years, more of my friends have walked, following their own path.

Fast-track senior executive John Reid left the Coca-Cola Company to pursue environmental and civic causes. Joe LaBonté, former president of Reebok International, resigned to spend more time on the West Coast, closer to his family, and to address social justice issues through his nonprofit organization.

Both returned to corporations later. John even returned to Coca-Cola for some environmental work. Neither was trying to downshift or seek voluntary simplicity. They left to do work more in tune with the words of writer Elbert Hubbard: "We work to become, not to acquire."

But most of my friends have not walked.

One, a partner at a top investment bank, recently managed a deal in which I was involved. We had a private lunch together before the transaction closed. I asked her about her life.

"I live on airplanes," she confided. "I make more than I could ever spend. But work is my whole world. I have no friends, never see my parents or brothers, and haven't had a date since I can remember.

"When I go on vacation, I almost always get called back. I know I will never have my own family [she's forty-two]. I've been ready for years to do something else, to be outdoors more, to feel more alive. But I don't know what else I would do, or really could do well. I feel empty."

She remains stuck in place.

Some companies insist on attendance at numerous company functions and get-togethers to make you *part of the family.* As one executive noted: "I've had it with working here. But how can I leave? All my friends are here. I couldn't leave *them.*"

We are the products of editing, rather than authorship.
—GEORGE WALD

At my fifteen-year college reunion in 1988, my classmates were asked to pinpoint the source of their happiness. As expected, the results strongly indicated the importance of family and community.

But among those who cited their work as the source of their happiness, nearly all reported that they had switched to "a career I never planned on earlier in my life."

A surprise? Not to me and not to my classmates. As management guru Peter Drucker said: "The probability that the first choice you make is right is roughly one in a million. If you decide your first choice is the right one, chances are you are just plain lazy."

By my twenty-fifth reunion in 1998, many of my classmates had been through midlife crises and major career shifts. This was particularly true of doctors, affected by managed care, and lawyers. Most transitions were soul-searching, but in time many had relaunched healthful, enjoyable careers.

Some had stayed within their professions, others had moved into political and social causes. Most important, their "new work" made them happy. In short, absorbing work—the right work, the kind that feels like play—always has been and always will be the spice of life.

To make it easier to change jobs, those who made a switch had kept their walking costs low, and they continued to do so. Their identification was not with a particular job or institution, but with doing work they found meaningful.

And guess what else? All those mountains they thought they saw in the distance—all those difficulties—turned out to be molehills.

Life is either a daring adventure or nothing at all.
—HELEN KELLER

Based in Battle Creek, Michigan, Tom Reis is currently the venture philanthropy director at the Kellogg Foundation, one of the five largest private foundations in the United States, boasting assets in excess of $6 billion. And his mission is no less than to "have a blast trying to turn the *Queen Mary* of philanthropy."

After years of living and learning from a vast array of jobs, he has finally perfected his own particular form of art—creating new ways to unleash resources for the public good. He hopes to create a new model of philanthropy to catalyze social entrepreneurs, socially minded business leaders, and emerging social investors.

He got where he is by never meeting a walking cost he didn't simply walk over.

For Tom Reis, life is an adventure, a series of adventures. He approaches it with an intensity of purpose, a dedication to making a difference. He is clear that he isn't really sure where he is going, but he does know where he has been.

Still, there was a time when moving from job to job—to keep growing, to keep contributing—wasn't easy for Tom. That's where his wife, Anne, came in—she of balance, she of insight, she of compassion. Yet Tom could not accept her permission to follow his own path until the internal conflict between his work life and his personal values became unbearable.

On that trip out west, he began his life anew.

> **If the things we believe are different than
> the things we do, there can be no true happiness.**
> —DANA TELFORD

Raised by hardworking, middle-class Catholic parents in Chicago and St. Paul, Minnesota, Tom Reis and his older sister were the "elders of the tribe" of five children.

She was the favorite of a corporate father who worked constantly; he was favored by a strong mother who volunteered constantly. His mother imbued her oldest son with the ideas of giving back or, as he calls it, "stewardship, a sense of responsibility."

Tom grew up with a strong work ethic. He mowed lawns, bagged groceries, and worked as a caddie at the nearby golf course. He also developed a sense of self-worth and confidence, which gave him a zest for taking risks and seeing exotic places.

Young Tom had an "unabashed passion for life and the gift of life."

"My passion grew from feeling I was dysfunctional at times, an outsider," Tom says. He made sure that attitude didn't waver when he felt that he fit in neither at his blue-collar Catholic boys school nor in his town.

From his earliest recollections, he thought little about a career or business. He just did what had to be done. He considered a career as "the de facto result of a series of experiences."

Tom did plan to go to Africa. That desire served as the catalyst that pushed him to discover life—everywhere.

Even so, his journey had its share of pain. Tom found life complicated. He was immature and not the "good altar-boy type." He worried about not being able to find "pat answers to the future."

More interested in the car he bought at sixteen, Tom didn't work that hard in school, but he did manage his time well— a result of his busy work schedule outside of school. College was a necessity in 1967. The alternative was the draft and a ticket to Vietnam.

A vocal antiwar teen, he still chose Notre Dame, a bastion of faith in God and country, over Berkeley, Dartmouth, and Georgetown. It was a bad choice: "All men. It was tough, and I was in deep trouble right away."

Not surprisingly, Tom was a misfit during his freshman year at Notre Dame. Compounding his discomfort, Tom found himself with no career plans in a sea of suits, people who knew exactly what they wanted to do not only next year, but for the next thirty years.

"I thought, Why isn't this clear to me? Why can't I just know that I want to do business or something? I was drinking. I was unhappy, and I had to stay in school."

**The best thing about the future
is that it comes only one day at a time.**
—ABRAHAM LINCOLN

All this distress pushed Tom into what he calls his "first great blind decision." He decided to "embrace the mystery stuff" and take for granted that "life is just full of wonder, waiting to happen for you. But you have to be flexible, open, and ready to follow it. I was ready."

Tom enrolled at Sophia University in Tokyo. It was the only year-abroad program he could find at Notre Dame that didn't require previous language training. There he got involved in a six-month university strike, found he could pick up languages easily, and became passionate about Japanese culture and alternatives to Catholicism. He also drank less.

Tom would return to Tokyo over the summers, working at the World's Fair, learning about "spaceship Earth"—"my emerging *global* responsibility to stewardship." His gift continued to be that he knew what he *didn't* want to do. It helped steer him to his second great blind decision.

After returning to Notre Dame and eventually graduating, Tom decided to join the Peace Corps. He understood that "the gift of life is the journey, not getting to the cabin." And he wanted to explore nature, culture, the world—in Africa, of course.

The Peace Corps didn't work out. Blind decision number three: After being turned down for Micronesia, he turned down Iran and South Korea.

Tom reflects: "I should have taken South Korea. I only had $1,000 to go to Europe with a friend. Africa was out of the question.

"But out of the blue, a neighborhood friend came through with a construction job I had been trying to get forever," he says, "and I was making $13 an hour. After six months I saved the $5,000 I needed to go where I wanted—Africa."

It is only with the heart one can see rightly.
What is essential is invisible to the eye.
—ANTOINE DE SAINT-EXUPÉRY

Tom was abroad for four years in Africa, Europe, and Latin America. His strategic plan amounted to this: Climb Mount Kilimanjaro. See Victoria Falls. Cross the Sahara.

"I'm glad we didn't overcook it. By not having a plan, by being on the great wheel of life, I let it happen to me," he says, "and it came at me full force.

"If you let it happen to you . . . that's your *control*. It isn't control over the experience, but control over the unexpected grace of the world as a learning laboratory."

Tom loved those four years and twenty-two African countries—even with three flies in his first sandwich, the horror of discovering no bark on the trees in southern Sudan (starving people had eaten it), poverty the likes of which he had never seen, and temperatures reaching 130 degrees Fahrenheit. He had a broader, deeper definition of his "spaceship Earth."

"Africa was my rite of passage, my coming of age as a man," he says. A stay in an African prison even provided a lesson in taking responsibility for others.

"I took the fall for a group of us. We were going native—swimming naked. I could have paid the $150 fine, but decided to take the thirty days."

A white-wigged magistrate put him in jail. Tom taught the prison guards math, became friendly with them, and, with a few dollars from his friend Charley, "escaped" four days later—back to Zambia.

Tom continued to put himself in the right places and simply let life happen to him. He taught English to "prolong my stay on this wonderful wheel of life." In 1974 he went to South America. In Quito, Ecuador, he would meet three women at a bookstore, one of whom was Anne, his future wife.

To be nobody but yourself, in a world
which is doing its best to make you everybody else,
means to fight the hardest battle which any
human being can fight, and never stop fighting.
—E. E. CUMMINGS

They returned to the United States in 1975, Anne to get her graduate degree in Tennessee. It was time for Tom to get a *real* job. He was twenty-six years old.

"I figured I would try Dad's corporate contacts," Tom recalls. "I went through four or five job interviews. They were disastrous. The more interviews I went to, the less effort I made to take an interest."

Just when he found himself unable even to feign interest, Tom was scheduled for an interview with the national sales manager at Pillsbury's headquarters in Minneapolis. His lack of attention to the questions he was asked intrigued the manager, who began to draw Tom out on a number of topics.

Finally he told Tom: "You may not know where you're going, but you know where you've been. That's more than I see with most people your age, and it will serve you and me well."

He hired Tom on the spot.

Tom Reis's story might have ended there. He did well. He got the promotions he sought. He and Anne married and settled into a big house in St. Paul. The new job required long hours and a lot of travel, but his compensation was "a ton of money."

Tom was on his way, but not the way expected. He was losing his life's energy. The drinking was the first sign.

On that national park trip out west five years into their Pillsbury life, Anne gave Tom "permission"—permission to leave the desert and go move mountains. Anne's response is more common than you might imagine.

**For this is the journey that men make: to find themselves.
If they fail in this, it doesn't matter much
what else they find.**
—JAMES A. MICHENER

Always a doer, never one to procrastinate, and rarely one to complain, Tom Reis moved on to a smaller company, Ringer, as vice president of sales and marketing. And he started doing a lot of volunteer work.

While he did not hate the work of his new job (he liked marketing and was good at it), he disliked the idea that this position was *it* for him—a worn path already trod by thousands before him.

Tom was afraid of being trapped, of not growing and contributing. He had a sense of disaffection with his environment, frustration over the lack of creativity, and a feeling of being out of control.

It was a gradual shift from Pillsbury—a journey done best a step at a time. And in that year, 1980, the drinking stopped.

It hasn't started again. "Once I stopped drinking, I reconnected with my higher power."

The creative juices started flowing again. He began volunteering on behalf of Cambodian and Hmong refugees in the Minneapolis/St. Paul area. That led to his next job offer, with a big cut in pay but a big gain of vacation time and a title as a faculty member at the University of Minnesota's Extension Service.

I don't know the key to success,
but the key to failure is trying to please everybody.
—BILL COSBY

Friends thought Tom was crazy even to think about the refugee project. "How could you do this?" they said. "How could you do this to your wife, Tom? You're insane to leave this great career."

But Anne thought it made sense. "We're not going to have as much money, that's all, and we'll have more time together," she said.

Tom walked. "As I began to take these turns in my career, gradually going beyond my concerns for money—helped substantially by Anne—I found my breadth of experience really made a difference. And," he adds, "it allowed me to begin pursuing causes, not money."

It went well.

Tom found he was "using marketing as I had never used it." He calls it "social marketing." He began to think about other ways to apply his commercial-sector skills for social good.

He liked the pace of life in the nonprofit sector. He liked the feeling that he could contribute some good in the world, and he realized that "the money didn't make that much difference."

The moral? You won't lose as much as you're afraid you will lose.

**Go confidently in the direction of your dreams.
Live the life you've imagined.**
—HENRY DAVID THOREAU

Tom and Anne began to think about having a family. Tom also felt he needed a graduate degree to open up more possibilities. Anne felt the same about her career.

So Anne and Tom both went through Harvard's Kennedy School midcareer program, the first couple to both attend the school and have a baby during school—between final exams.

As for their financial situation, they sold their St. Paul home at a $25,000 loss, quit their jobs, and began the Kennedy program in Cambridge, Massachusetts, just a month after confirming Anne's pregnancy. They had only enough money to last the year.

They grew used to being financially strapped. As Tom quotes Francis Bacon, "Riches are a good handmaid, but the worst mistress."

The birth of their daughter, Elizabeth, focused Tom's mind wonderfully. Now he knew he "wanted to build a longer-term strategy for work in general," he says, "and I knew it was going to revolve around the social sector. I also knew I would use a lot of commercial-sector management tools in iconoclastic ways in the social sector."

The Reises wanted to go overseas and were ready to go when an attractive job offer appeared from back home in St. Paul: deputy county administrator. The post came with a good salary, responsibility, a staff of two thousand, and a $29 million budget. It also had an established career path and security.

Tom walked away from the offer . . . with only $1,000 in the bank and a family to support. Doing so "helped me gain clarity," he says. "I could have gone that route, with regular salary increases and a life planned out for years to come. But it wasn't what we had in mind."

Moving on is a gift you give yourself.
—JOAN RIVERS

More fortune and "great blind decisions" followed Tom and his family, now with son Colin in tow.

They spent five years in Indonesia—four in provincial Java, one in Jakarta—working on a large public health project. Tom used his newly developed social marketing techniques to help educate mothers dealing with diarrhea and dehydration. He also promoted family planning and designed health education programs to improve nutrition and complete immunization efforts.

"It was the most rewarding work I've ever done. I was so happy there. I know for a fact I personally saved some children's lives."

Tom and the family flourished. "We had a leisurely lifestyle. We were grounded in a fascinating place with many cultures. We became fluent in another language. I was able to come home for lunch every day and be with the kids. We had a great time and a great career."

Yet Anne and Tom knew that they eventually had to leave to give a sense of their home culture to their children, Elizabeth and Colin.

Also, Tom didn't want to get "stuck overseas and into an expatriate rut."

Senior staff at the Kellogg Foundation asked him to speak to them on his ideas about social marketing programs. At least, that was what Tom thought.

What he found was that Kellogg was interested in having him join the foundation, to apply his ideas about social marketing to their work. The foundation president had worked with Tom before, when they were at the University of Minnesota. Now their paths were crossing again. By coincidence? Tom signed on.

Sometimes when I consider
what tremendous consequences come from little things . . .
I am tempted to think . . . there are no little things.
—RALPH WALDO EMERSON

Tom left the villages of Indonesia, where he could see the immediate impact of his actions, and joined colleagues who had been academics and community activists. They looked on marketing as somewhat crass and only vaguely relevant.

At Kellogg, Tom had to earn respect internally before he could even begin to do what he really wanted to do at the foundation: to bring fundamental change to the process of foundation grant making.

"'Career' is still a word that's foreign to me. Work is just what I do for other reasons—to try to have fun and to do some good. Actually, having fun for me *is* doing good; it's contributing.

"But it's also true that there are some opportunities I want to pursue at Kellogg that could bring about real change." And change, of course, is something Tom Reis appreciates. "I think of all the turns our Land Rover took in Africa years ago. It's the same in my career."

What about Anne? Today, when Tom weighs a decision, Anne simply asks, "Will it mean more time with the family?" On their list of life criteria, money has fallen on hard times. They now rank it in fifth place, way behind their top priorities.

The truth is, the Reis family may walk away from money, but never from living a life out loud.

Destiny is not a matter of chance, but a matter of choice.
It is not a thing to be waited for,
it is a thing to be achieved.
—WILLIAM JENNINGS BRYAN

❋

Lifelines

As career coach Marjorie Blanchard warned, "If you are not working on your ideal day, you are working on someone else's."

I sometimes wonder what the world would be like if no one had a job they didn't want to do, if people didn't get really good at things they no longer wanted to do.

If you are asking yourself, "What happened to me?" are you prepared to quit your job? Now? Most of us are not.

We may not be able to control many forces of employment, but we can control our own employability by being flexible and focused. Being flexible means gradually lowering your walking costs. It means being careful not to build a lifestyle or expectations that make a transition difficult. To overcome potential loss and ease the transition, have friends and activities outside your workplace and industry, and develop an identity outside of work.

It's never too late to be what we could have been, to seek a newer world. As noted French hostess and woman of letters Madame du Deffand once said, "The distance is nothing; it is only the first step which is difficult."

For Tom Reis, it took the pain of alcoholism and the affirmation of his wife to begin living the adult life he wanted to live. Often we don't trust our spouses, family members, and real friends to help us see the light.

When Tom finally made the move, he found that, as Mark

Twain quipped, "I've had a lot of problems in my life, and most of them never happened."

In the end, it is important to remember that we cannot become what we need to be by remaining what we are.
—MAX DE PREE

CHAPTER 3

✹

TAKE YOUR PLACE
AT THE TABLE OF LIFE

Judy Wicks's Ministry

**In him to whom love dwells,
the whole world is but one family.**
—GAUTAMA BUDDHA

My humanity is bound up in yours,
for we can only be human together.
—Bishop Desmond Tutu

I enjoy our synagogue. We found a rabbi whose values of inclusion and interconnectedness of all peoples, all religions, are similar to ours. Interfaith activities are ongoing, weekly events. There is no "we," no "they." There is only us.

He has created a sacred space that fills us with community, that fills us with a stronger sense of ourselves. We are inspired to *tikun olam*—to make the world a better place.

It is precious to find that space in the world, whether in a religious setting, on a mountaintop, at home, or work, or wherever it may be. It is a space we carry with us wherever we go, whatever we do.

I am reminded of this space by the story of three African men answering the question How can you tell when night ends and day begins?

The first man responds: "When I can distinguish the olive trees from the fig trees, then I know that night is over and day has begun."

The second man answers: "When I can see the forms of the animals across the Serengeti, I know that the darkness is leaving and the light of day arriving."

Finally, a man renowned for his wisdom replies: "When we see a black woman and a white woman and call them both 'sister,' when we see a poor man and a rich man and call them both 'brother,' then the darkness of night has lifted and the light of day has come."

TAKE YOUR PLACE AT THE TABLE OF LIFE

We are here to help one another along life's journey.
—WILLIAM BENNETT

When I was twenty-two I spent the winter in Goa, India, then a beach community that attracted young fugitives from Western values. There I met Gary, a twenty-eight-year-old Canadian who had made millions of dollars in real estate. Gary had one of Goa's few luxurious houses, replete with stereo systems and automobiles. He also had a wealth of food and drink.

Gary shared with everyone. My first week there, a young Frenchman totaled Gary's Jeep. No problem, Gary said.

During the next week, Gary and I took a walk on the beach. I wanted to know why someone as seemingly smart as Gary let all these hippies take advantage of him.

"I share because it makes me feel good to see others enjoy what I have been lucky enough to gain," he told me.

"Take advantage of me? How can anyone take advantage of you if you are doing what you want? You are giving me an opportunity to share. Remember Gandhi's words: 'You can fulfill everyone's need, but not one man's greed.'"

Gary's words left me baffled for the next fifteen years.

Judy Wicks has since taught me the lessons I was not yet ready to learn from Gary. A remarkable person, Judy is founder and presiding maître d' of Philadelphia's famous White Dog Cafe and its retail outlet, the Black Cat.

Judy is a walking monument to the pleasures of sharing. She wants every one of our planet's six billion people to have a seat at the table of life—a table of dignity, respect, and hope. No one is denied a place. And she has developed a $4.3 million-a-year business that nets well above the industry average to exemplify that table.

For Judy Wicks, "my business is my ministry."

Ear cocked to the world, Judy learned sooner than I did

about synchronicity. About being in tune with one another. About being in tune with nature. All share. There's plenty for everyone.

At fifty Judy Wicks has defined her life in terms of inclusion—the interconnectedness of all beings, the harmony of male/female, young/old, white/black, rich/poor, U.S./foreign. Not surprisingly, she started on this path after an encounter with exclusion.

Experience is not what happens to you.
It's what you do with what happens to you.
—ALDOUS HUXLEY

Growing up in Ingomar, Pennsylvania, just outside Pittsburgh, Judy played baseball at an early age with her lawyer father, an ardent baseball fan. She recalls her excitement on hearing that her fifth-grade class was about to form a baseball team.

As she raced onto the field for the first day of practice, Judy was told to "go over there" to practice cheerleading. Only boys could play ball.

She still remembers standing behind the backstop, watching the boys play, feeling contempt for herself and for her girlfriends—second-class citizens.

"I learned what discrimination felt like and what it does. I was a good ballplayer. We would have done much better with me in there. When you leave people out of the game, you aren't hurting just them. You're hurting yourself and the whole group."

Judy never did lead cheers, or play baseball, although she did later marry the best fifth-grade player. She grew quiet in the classroom and, for many years, struggled to recapture her fourth-grade enthusiasm.

We are all angels with one wing,
able to fly only when we embrace each other.
—ANONYMOUS

For Judy Wicks, spirituality—and her place in the world—is exhibited in her relationships with other people, people of all colors, all socioeconomic classes.

"I don't go to church," she says. "I don't pray. I went as a child, saw no signs, and just never thought about God until a few years ago. A friend who loves to garden mentioned that, one day, a beautiful butterfly landed on her hand. That was her moment of pure joy.

"One night I was on the street outside the restaurant, surrounded by people, putting on one of our annual events, dancing to a good Motown song. I looked around me, saw the faces of my customers, a real racially diverse group of urbanites out there around midnight dancing in the street, and I just looked into those faces and found this profound sense of joy.

"It was my moment of pure joy.

"God is in the faces of my customers. For me, spirituality and business are related. It is really through my business that I express my love for other people and my sense of interconnectedness with the world.

"I use my business as a way of building my own capacity to care, and building the capacity of my customers and my staff to care. That is what I mean when I call it my ministry."

As much as anyone I know, Judy walks the talk. She uniquely integrates work, family, and community in a world of joyous, playful love, with a serious underlying commitment to social activism. When I speak of building a little community of those you love and who love you, Judy is my example.

- With her children, Grace and Lawrence, committed in their own ways to social activism.

- On Sansom Street, location of her home and business, where she fought successfully to keep the historic brownstones intact.
- In the city of Philadelphia, where the press calls Judy "a great Philadelphia treasure" and says: "If everyone in Casablanca knew Rick [Humphrey Bogart], it seems that everyone in Philadelphia knows Judy." Judy takes her customers to other "sister" restaurants that are owned by minorities within inner-city communities.
- In the world community, her "Table for Six Billion, Please!" and "Eating with the Enemy" programs fly customers to sister restaurants in Nicaragua, Cuba, Vietnam, and the like for food combined with thought about how our differences are far less than our similarities.

> **A man is only as good as what he loves.**
> —SAUL BELLOW

I start many speeches to MBAs with a film about Judy's business activism. It is an inspiring story of someone who has found herself, her place, her success in life. It is what Judy calls "being able to act on what I really care about."

It took time, patience, and much work. She listened and learned . . . a bit at a time. The result is a place in harmony with both her nature and her principles.

Yet the reaction of my MBA audiences is almost always the same: "What a national franchise!" they exclaim. "Another Cheers [the Boston bar of television fame, "where everybody knows your name"], a place of song and community in a lonely world, with the fun and joy of drinks like the White Dog's Leg-Lifter Lager. Can I call her and buy a franchise for my city?"

"A no-brainer," I'm told, with Judy's fame and business formula: great food, soft-touch service, friendly atmosphere, community-building talk programs nightly at which locals and world leaders share their life stories at one of her "Table Talks."

And her quarterly newsletter, *Tales from the White Dog Cafe,* read by eighteen thousand Philadelphians; her high school mentoring programs; her community tours—what a great way to build a national chain, city by city, each with its own White Dog Cafe. "Then," I'm told, "the White Dog could go global."

To such a suggestion, Judy would simply smile, let out one of her sharp staccato laughs to hint you're out of bounds, and answer: "I'm a 'small is beautiful' kind of a person. Growing the business in that way is not my interest. Rather than growing larger, I prefer to go deeper with what I have. I prefer to ask, How can I have deeper, more profound relationships with those around me—my staff, my customers, my local community, the farmers who grow our food, the farmers who grow our coffee in Mexico? That's what interests me.

"Most of the world's problems—and the problems people have figuring out who they are, where they fit in the world—would be solved if people understood their part in something bigger than themselves," she would conclude.

Judy runs a business that expresses who she is. What Judy believes is exhibited in the way she lives, loves, and laughs: "My business is largely guided by my passions. I love food and parties . . . and the concept of interconnectedness. What I do—what I enjoy doing—is to use good food to lure innocent customers into social activism."

Judy wants to expand the White Dog and Black Cat. It wouldn't be a geographical expansion. It would be an expansion of her community programs anchored by one profitable "good, great eating place." After fifteen years the list of community programs already takes up three full pages, single-spaced.

Judy's motivation is to include, to share: "If the powerful institution of business is directed toward involving everyone in the game, maybe there will someday be a world where everyone has a place at the table. What a great party that would be!"

(Never doubt Judy's ability to throw a good party. Each Fourth of July she dresses up as a pregnant colonial woman with a sign on her back reading "George Washington Slept Here!" She gives "birth" to twins on the street, in front of hundreds of her partying customers and staff, when a midwife delivers black and white girls named Liberty and Justice, who jump up and tap-dance to "Yankee Doodle Dandy." The crowd lights sparklers and sings "God Bless America." It's quintessential Judy Wicks.)

> **Cherish forever what makes you unique,**
> **'cuz you're really a yawn if it goes.**
> —BETTE MIDLER

Bringing people together around food was a tradition in the Wicks family. Judy's parents hosted Friday night "Hungry Clubs" for friends. Grandmother Grace ran a guest house, and elegant Nana Eleanor taught Judy about service.

But typical of a 1947-born boomer—emulate and rebel— Judy rejected home economics in school, preferring woodworking class. When she was prohibited from taking shop, she jumped out of a classroom window to avoid learning how to cook and sew.

Judy's parents took her camping, so she did learn campfire cooking. At five she hooked up a record player in her driveway and set up her first "restaurant." A neighborhood boy, notable for his big feet and ears, was her first customer.

For the next several years Judy kept trying different businesses and building different things—a practice she continues at the White Dog. She sold wood objects from her wagon, built a miniature golf course in the woods and charged kids a nickel to play, directed all the group games, organized a theater group, started an adventure club and a bike club, and built the clubhouses.

After the baseball incident, Judy became shy in the classroom, hardly ever raising her hand. In her mainly white, conservative town, Judy's worldly knowledge was limited. Upon hearing of a man named "Silverberg," she asked if he was a full-blooded American Indian.

Judy went off to Ohio, to what she calls "Lake College for Erie Women" (actually Lake Erie College). At this small, insulated school, even as the Vietnam War led to disruptive protests on many campuses, Judy's only political involvement was a sit-in to allow the girls to put their feet on the coffee tables in the library. They won that one.

After graduation in 1969, Judy married her grade-school boyfriend, Dick Hayne, the best baseball player on the fifth-grade team that Judy once longed to join. The newlyweds decided to enlist in VISTA and went off to live in an Eskimo village in Alaska.

Judy's second profound learning experience was about to begin.

Snowflakes are one of nature's most fragile things, but just look at what they can do when they stick together.
—VESTA KELLY

As Judy recalls: "I learned so much from living with indigenous people. In a harsh environment like Alaska, there was a natural communal society, where individuals depended on the strength of the group and acted in ways that supported the whole rather than profiting at the expense of others.

"When you admire something an Eskimo has, they give it to you," Judy says. "They don't believe in accumulating more than their neighbor."

In the spring, for example, when a man catches his first seal after a long hard winter, his wife throws a seal party for the entire village. She divides the seal meat equally among all the women and gives away other treasures accumulated during the year—buttons, pieces of cloth, and so forth. The hostess tosses the items in the air, and the women catch them in their skirts.

"They don't believe in competition," says Judy. "They don't believe in envy. They believe in sharing."

The Eskimo culture was completely alien to twenty-two-year-old Judy's experience in a society that "rewards people for being greedy," and it was profoundly revealing.

"I came to the realization that a successful and sustainable economy is one based not on hoarding, but on sharing; not on excluding, but on finding a way for everyone to play the game according to their individual strengths and interests."

Love each other or perish.
—W. H. AUDEN

Judy is reminded of a story she first heard from her friend Ben Cohen, of Ben & Jerry's Homemade, Inc., about the difference between heaven and hell.

In both places people live in large banquet halls replete with food and song. Everyone is required to use utensils for eating . . . but the utensils are so long that it is impossible to use them to get food into one's mouth. Unless people can somehow grow longer arms, it seems everyone will go hungry. In hell they are all starving and miserable. However, in heaven everyone is full and happy, because each person is feeding another.

Judy and Dick left Alaska, using the $3,000 they received from VISTA to co-found an alternative clothing store in Philadelphia.

The Free People Store grew from a low-margin, "let's just make enough to eat" enterprise into what would become Urban Outfitters—a highly successful national chain, which Dick continues to run today.

But at twenty-four years old, just a year after the store opened, Judy realized that something was missing from her life, something the little girl who loved to play baseball once had and lost. She decided to leave both the business and the marriage in order to find it.

Judy felt guilty about the divorce: "It's all my fault." No one had ever been divorced in her family. So she did nothing to look out for her own interests.

I've climbed the ladder of success, wrong by wrong.
—MAE WEST

Making her getaway in an old station wagon, Judy promptly ran a red light only half a block from the store and crashed into another car.

A passerby who stopped to help got an earful on Judy's plight. It had taken all her strength just to pack up and leave. How could she turn back now?

"Listen," this Good Samaritan said to Judy, "I work in this French restaurant, La Terrasse, and they need a waitress. Why don't you take the job?"

That was how Judy Wicks got into the restaurant business—quite literally by accident.

She went from novice waitress to general manager, increasing revenue tenfold in ten years and turning La Terrasse into a moneymaker. But her partnership with the restaurant's owner was less successful.

Judy just "assumed that people would appreciate my work and realize I was valuable—that they needed me. It didn't work that way." And she didn't have a written contract.

Undaunted, Judy opened a tiny muffin shop in 1983, just down the street from La Terrasse, on the first floor of the brownstone she and her second husband, an architect, had bought together.

The marriage dissolved after fifteen years, but there were welcome by-products: Grace in 1979 and Lawrence in 1981. Soon Judy was expanding outside her family, too, adding soups and breads to her muffin shop, going from one room to the building next door, from takeout to a two-hundred-seat restaurant.

Finally, this time, Judy made sure that the restaurant was hers—no partners until chef Kevin von Klause, who joined her in 1986, got a 5 percent stake.

Do not seek to follow in the footsteps of the men of old. Seek what they sought.
—BASHO

Just after moving into what are now the five brownstones on 3420 Sansom Street—her restaurant, gift shop, and home—Judy learned that her residence once housed the famous Russian spiritualist Helena Blavatsky. This discovery led to the naming of the White Dog Cafe.

To combat a serious illness in 1875, Madame Blavatsky's doctors wanted to amputate her leg. But she insisted on keeping all her body parts intact. Otherwise, she is said to have quipped, "when I die, my obituary could read: 'Gone to meet her leg.'"

Spurning surgery, Madame Blavatsky instead had a white dog lie across her ailing leg. As legend has it, the leg was miraculously healed.

Madame Blavatsky traveled the world in search of enlightenment, including, she said, a seven-year stint in India studying with Hindu mahatmas. In the United States, where she also studied American Indian mysticism, Blavatsky was best known for founding the Theosophical Society, a group dedicated to uniting all nations and religions through a common understanding of ethical truths.

In a word, Blavatsky preached interdependence. When asked what religion she believed in, she replied, "All of them."

Judy's White Dog Cafe has a proud heritage.

> **With stammering lips and insufficient sounds,**
> **I strive and struggle to deliver right**
> **the music of my nature . . .**
> —ELIZABETH BARRETT BROWNING

The demise of her second marriage left Judy with twice the debt, but not in doubt about what she wanted to do in life. The White Dog was her creation. She would turn it into the kind of business she envisaged. But no great light suddenly dawned about what to do. The White Dog's mix of activism and economics happened gradually.

Nor was it all smooth sailing—far from it. "For the first five years," says Judy, "I was just trying to keep my head above water. Then I started giving fund-raisers for causes I believed in. Next I thought up the sister restaurant project.

"It began as a pen pal project, but then one of my customers convinced me to go to Nicaragua to find the sister restaurant myself. That started it all," Judy declares.

But it was the difficulty of doing it all that pushed Judy toward integrating her life and her business. Lacking the time for both her nonprofit and her business activities, Judy brought the two together.

Integrating her children into her business was actually easier. Before the Industrial Revolution, most people worked at home, running the farm, the inn, the shop. There was little chance to leave your values at home and go to work. So, too, with Judy. She lives right above the White Dog and Black Cat.

"I think Marie Wilson's [Ms. Foundation] 'Take Your Daughters [Children] to Work' program is great," begins Judy. "But that was never a problem for me.

"Two days after Grace was born, I took her to the restaurant. At night I put her on top of the piano while we cleaned up. We finished, and I went home and crawled into bed. Something felt funny. Hmm. What was it? I screamed, 'The baby's missing!'

"I ran back to the restaurant. There she was, still asleep on the piano. So, you see, my problem is not bringing my children to work, but remembering to bring them home."

**When shall we learn that we are all related
one to the other, that we are all members of one body?**
—HELEN KELLER

Albert Einstein was fascinated by Mahatma Gandhi. He watched newsreel after newsreel of Gandhi's doings in India. Having seen Gandhi greet people in the street with his hands placed together as if in prayer, and with a bow, Einstein wondered what Gandhi was saying (newsreels had no sound in those days).

Einstein wrote to Gandhi, who replied: *"Namastay."* Einstein then wrote again to ask the meaning of this Hindu word *namastay.*

Gandhi responded: "I honor the place in you where the entire universe resides. I honor the place in you of light, love, truth, peace, and wisdom. I honor the place in you where, when you are in that place, and I am in that place, there's only one of us."

Judy Wicks's philosophy of life jelled in her fiftieth year when she listened to an audiotape about the life of Gandhi.

People wondered why a spiritual leader would involve himself so deeply in politics and economics. Gandhi felt the answer was simple. He didn't believe in separating spirituality (family), economics (business), and politics (social activism). Neither does mother, businesswoman, and social activist Judy Wicks.

> **My objective in life is not to have a spiritual life**
> **that is separate from the rest of my life.**
> —ED MCCRACKEN

Judy speaks proudly, at times almost defiantly, of how she has created a successful business and brought her values to bear at the same time. She sees spirituality as rooted in social activism. Compartmentalization and separation are dangerous on all accounts.

Her arguments often rely on good business sense.

"Everyone is always trying to find out, 'How can my business be different from someone else's? How can my business be unusual?' Well, don't look too far," Judy advises, "because the way your business can be unusual is by having it reflect yourself. Everybody is different, and if your business actually reflects you as an individual, it's going to be different. My business is who I am."

Who is Judy Wicks? In her words, she is a global citizen dedicated to "peace through parties." She exemplifies the integration and has fun doing it.

Judy is just as likely to jump on your table at a slightly stodgy dinner party and begin barking (with appropriate dog nose and face painting—I have it on video!) as she is to engage you to accompany her on a business trip to Mexico to support the rights of indigenous peoples. Not only her staff, but also her customers go on these activist trips, because they buy into the White Dog's brand of values.

"People come to the White Dog because they're hungry," asserts Judy. "But they're hungry not just for food. People in our society hunger for other things. They hunger to share their values, for a sense of community, and to be part of something that is larger than themselves."

A good local example is Judy's mentoring program with students from the Restaurant, Hotel, and Tourism Academy at West Philadelphia High School. Students are mentored by the White Dog staff and go on field trips to family farms, sister restaurants, and vendors to see minority-owned businesses in action.

How did it all start?

We discover ourselves through others.
—CARL JUNG

"In 1992 I was driving by the local high school and saw kids coming out, all African American. I thought, This is my neighborhood school, and I don't know one of them. I don't know anything about them. I want to know who they are." So she challenged herself to find out.

Judy called the high school principal and began the mentoring program. Later she added a college scholarship and an annual event.

Recently at the year-end, intergenerational, interracial Hip Hop, which the students put together along with Judy's staff, a young man named David showed up with his girlfriend, bringing hugs and joy. David is attending college, funded in part by Judy and the White Dog.

As he walked over to Judy to give her a hug, tears welled in her eyes. "I have finally figured out who those children are that I saw coming out of the high school that day," she says. "They are our own children."

For Judy, this was her third profound experience. "It made

me think that society does not have so much of a problem with loving its own children as with loving other people's children. Shouldn't we do our best to love them as our own?

"So many friends of mine are worried more about whether their children go to Yale than the fact that many other children are going to jail. Maybe we should be more concerned with the fate of all children."

In the early 1990s 25 percent of black youths were in jail or on parole; by the late 1990s the number had grown to 33 percent. Judy has been able to address social ills like this by integrating activism into her business. For someone who "missed the entire civil rights movement," it wasn't easy—or planned.

Everybody can be great . . . because *anybody* can serve.
You don't have to have a college degree to serve. You
don't have to make your subject and verb agree to serve.
You only need a heart full of grace.
A soul generated by love.
—DR. MARTIN LUTHER KING JR.

When Judy Wicks gets up each morning, she goes right to her closet, opens it, and reads her sign that says "Good Morning, Beautiful Business."

"I put it there because it reminds me of how beautiful business is when we see it as a way of really expressing our love for others. We see the great promise of business: to provide opportunity for everyone. To link the energy and power of business with the energy and power of love and compassion for other people."

As the White Dog and Judy have become increasingly well-known the past few years, opportunities to address important social problems have multiplied. Judy has been enlisted by President Clinton as an activist who has a business leader's credibility. She has fought for the America she believes in, a country of peace and a country that does the right things.

On November 16, 1997, Judy Wicks was arrested for her first act of civil disobedience. She was incarcerated after going to Georgia as part of a White Dog delegation of customers and staff protesting the U.S. government's training of Latin American militia in Georgia. Judy proudly recounts the event: "As I marched toward detention, I had never felt so free. In disobeying, I had never followed my country's ideals more truly. In being present in the moment, I had never stood more clearly for what I believe, nor felt more profoundly the interconnectedness of our world."

It was a far cry from feet on coffee tables.

**We can do no great things,
only small things with great love.**
—MOTHER TERESA

It took years and a lot of living for the seeds planted in the youthful experiences of Judy Wicks to grow to their full realization. When she put it together, she found her special space—to contribute, to make a life while making a living.

As Judy notes: "It's all about balance. At the heart of it is the integration of my community life with my business life. I never go too far in either direction. Too much focus on profit is no good; neither is too much social activism while ignoring profit. Capitalism for the common good, community action for economic strength—two sides of one coin. That's what nourishes me and my business."

Judy has created Business for Fair Trade and Human Rights in Chiapas, an ad hoc group of sixteen American chief executive officers whose companies import Mexican products. Organized in response to violence against the pro-democracy movement in Mexico, they intend to protect the rights of indigenous people from whom the group buys products.

After the December 1997 massacre of indigenous people in Chiapas, Judy and her group held a press conference in Mexico City. A reporter from *Progresso,* the Mexican equivalent of *Time,* asked, "Is your group about human rights or is it about business?"

"It's about both," Judy replied.

Mystified, the reporter pressed for clarification: "Both? How?"

"That's the point," Judy said. "You can do business and support human rights, the environment, and fair trade. All at once."

When you cease to make a contribution, you begin to die.
—ELEANOR ROOSEVELT

It's a point Judy Wicks proves to the world every day of her life, as she takes her place at the universal table of life—a table of life and work nourishing each other entirely in sync, harmonious.

In keeping with her trademark "Table for Six Billion, Please!" Judy concludes, "Imagine that there is one big world table where everyone is sitting. I can see ourselves joining hands, offering this grace:

Heavenly Father, Mother of our Earth, Universal Spirit who dwells here in each of our hearts, forgive us for the harm we have done to our planet and the plants and animals who live here with us. Forgive us the harm we have caused each other.

Thank you for giving us the courage to put aside our fears of not having enough for ourselves, so that we could make room for every one of us around this table of great abundance and nourishment.

Thank you for the creativity it has taken to find ways for each of us to participate in the making of this great feast, so that we can each join in the satisfaction of our work well done.

Bless this food that we now eat with the greatest joy, knowing that you are present in the pleasure of every bite, and in the love we see all around us in each and every smiling face. Amen.

I have a dream that one day, on the red hills of Georgia, the sons of former slaves and the sons of former slaveowners will be able to sit down together at the table of brotherhood.
—DR. MARTIN LUTHER KING JR.

✳

Lifelines

Judy Wicks's story asks you to look around yourself, at the people and activities in your life. Are you in the place you want to be? Are you working with—living with—people you admire and respect? Are you in sync?

Zen master Hsueh-Feng once said, "The whole world is you. Yet you keep thinking there is something else." Often we fail to realize how we create the world around us in so many ways.

Finding your place in the world is not easy, however. The clues may be all around you, but you don't see or hear them. Friends, spouses, and co-workers may see you more clearly than you see yourself. (Ask them!)

As the ancient Zen masters professed, "Knock on the sky and listen to the sound."

Judy Wicks listened to the "teachable moments" in her life, applying the lessons of inclusion and interconnectedness that came from sports, Eskimos, and high school neighbors. They taught her how to grow a business and a life that resonates with her unique gifts and caring for the world.

As for the outside world, you will be confronted by what you see. And what you see is primarily what you look at.
—Zen saying

PART 2

WHAT DO YOU WANT?

Establish Purpose

CHAPTER 4

✳

KNOW HOW <u>YOU</u> MEASURE SUCCESS

Elliot Hoffman's Calling

———————

Try not to be a man of success, but a man of value.
—ALBERT EINSTEIN

The search for that personal definition of success . . .
is really a search for oneself.
—CHARLES HANDY

In June 1970 I had just finished my first year at college when my father arrived to celebrate his twenty-fifth reunion. The reunion was an opportunity for him to find out what was up with his eldest. He had every reason to wonder. Whereas he had left college after twelve months to fight a war in Europe, his son was protesting in the streets of Cambridge, in the United States.

Dad and I were close in those days. We spent time together walking and talking. We stopped on the Weeks Bridge, which spans the Charles River and connects the college with the business school. Dad was in a reflective mood.

"You ought to decide what you're going to strive for in life," he began. "For example, do you want to become rich, or do you want to become famous? Or maybe both—that's what everybody wants. But often it comes down to one or the other. Which will you choose to pursue?"

I didn't know.

Seeing my face on the cover of *Time* magazine seemed more in tune with what I wanted than having a big bag of bucks. But I really wasn't sure.

Fame or fortune; which should I pursue?

Like a tedious houseguest who won't go home, that question lingered in the back of my mind for the next twenty-six years. I couldn't get rid of it, couldn't make a choice.

**God will not ask how many books you have read,
how many miracles you have worked. He will ask you
if you have done your best, for the love of Him.**
—MOTHER TERESA

In June 1996 I was at a United Nations conference of twenty-five thousand people in Istanbul, Turkey. Meeting people from around the world, I began to realize how similar our desires were, that in many ways we were all dreaming the same dream. And once I realized that, the quintessential question suddenly seemed simple.

I finally knew how to answer my father's question the way I wanted to answer it.

It was the wrong question.

After all those years of climbing, trying to reach the summit, I now knew it was the wrong mountain—at least, for me. The question was: In a world of dreams shared, how could I make a life worth living?

The child is father of the man.
—WILLIAM WORDSWORTH

"How would you answer Grandpa's question today, Daddy? What would it be, money or fame?"

That from my eleven-year-old daughter, Amanda, who unhesitatingly offered her own view.

"I think it's pretty simple. I'd rather be rich because then I could give all my money to people who needed it. You can't give away fame."

Child teaches parent.

Success isn't about how much you have. It is about how much you give away.

Researchers see middle adulthood as offering people the

opportunity to renounce the "tyranny of the dream" and to become successful on more meaningful terms. As Dr. Daniel Levinson commented in *The Seasons of a Man's Life,* "When a man no longer feels he must be remarkable, he is more free to be himself and work according to his own wishes and talents."

Friends often tell me that I've helped them get at their "happiness."

When I advised one friend not to grow his business, he said he felt truly happy and at peace for the first time. The tyranny of the dream of success—doing, having, and winning more—was what had pushed him toward growth.

But looking deeply at his needs—to serve more and to be there more for his family, his community, and himself—he realized that business growth alone was, for him, an empty goal. It would actually prevent his success.

We have a need to be good, to be moral agents. Yet we can easily lose touch with what it feels like to be good, to be accepted, to feel that our lives matter.

> **It's just that fame and fortune ought to add up**
> **to more than just fame and fortune.**
> —ROBERT FULGHUM

Swedish chemist Alfred Nobel made his fortune by inventing dynamite and licensing his formula to governments. When his brother Ludwig died, a prominent newspaper mistakenly ran Alfred's obituary. It said he had made a fortune by helping armies around the world be more efficient at death and destruction.

Shocked and disgusted by his apparent legacy, Nobel decided to devote his fortune to humanitarian purposes. He established the Nobel Prize in the arts and sciences.

The founder of the Polaroid Corporation, Edwin Land,

believed that "the ultimate bottom line is in heaven." On this earth, we hunger to live a life of joyful purpose.

Nowhere does purpose or success seem as clear-cut or as joyful as in the world of sports—a world that influences our values, our notion of "hero." In our eyes, athletic success occurs in a distinct moment, a now of victory that can be easily measured.

But if you listen to some great athletes, you learn that they look at success in a more profound way than do spectators. In the words of Phil Jackson, the coach of the six-time world champion Chicago Bulls basketball team: "It is not the winning or losing that's important . . . it's the dance between you and your teammates, between you and your competitors. Don't even think of them as your opponents; they're your partners in the dance."

> **I do not try to dance better than anyone else.**
> **I only try to dance better than myself.**
> —MIKHAIL BARYSHNIKOV

While watching the 1976 Montreal Summer Olympics on television, I saw a ten-minute segment on Russian super-heavyweight weight lifter Vasili Alekseyev, arguably one of the greatest athletes of all time in any sport.

Year after year this sensitive, gentle giant—Vasili weighed in at 345 pounds—simply kept breaking his own records. He had all the honors and financial rewards Moscow could bestow. Why did he keep training and working so hard for so little?

The television reporter, recounting the great athlete's more than one hundred world records, put the question to him.

Sitting next to his beloved chessboard, with a favorite book of poetry by his side, Vasili spoke of purpose, of what he called "the white light." He lives for that "moment's moment" when he reaches a sense of perfection, a time of peace and harmony with himself, with others, with life itself.

"When I am ready to lift more weight than any man has ever done before, I visualize the moment when my arms will be lifted straight into the air, with the weight moving toward the sky. As I stand there in front of all those people, we are all together, knowing what has happened, that I have been able to do something that no one, not even myself, has been able to do before.

"At the instant when I feel the weight rising, and know I will make it, that instant is one of pure joy. Once I have lifted that weight, I let out my sound, and I am bathed in a sudden flash of white light. It comes from inside my brain, inside all of me, and sends a feeling through me of indescribable joy, true contentment.

"I work hundreds of hours in the gym each month, hoping to have a chance to experience that white light one more time. That wish fills me with happiness each day in the gym. It is my quiet. It is my peace. It is my knowing I have a purpose in this world."

I don't want to be rich. I just want to be loved.
—MARILYN MONROE

Elliot Hoffman's life is not as openly dramatic as Vasili Alekseyev's, but it is no less loving.

Nearly twenty years ago, Elliot, who operates a multicultural San Francisco food business called Just Desserts, instituted full maternity and paternity leave for all employees, including those who weren't married. He decided decades ago that all of his bakery and café employees—and their entire households—should have full dental and medical insurance. In his view they were entitled to the same protection he had.

Elliot gives much thought to those "left out of this economy" as well. When the cold war ended, he was among the first U.S. entrepreneurs to hire Soviet immigrants.

He also began the now nationally known Garden Project that employs parolees, among others, and is notable for having cultivated many lives along with the organic vegetables. Several of the project's once troubled alumni have gone on to productive work at Just Desserts and elsewhere. Some have even regained custody of their children.

Much of Elliot's life has been shaped by his own personal definition of success. He recalls one memorable lesson from a six-month college stint working in the securities analysis department at Manufacturers Hanover Trust.

"I saw these guys in their twenties who every twenty minutes would run over and check the stock ticker—as if they were tied to it by an umbilical cord! I remember thinking: Why are they doing this? It seemed they were measuring their success, their value, by what the stock tape said. . . . That's what was meaningful for their lives."

This is also a man who, wanting to get some extended time with his children before they were grown, took a year off at the height of his company's success. He has distinct views about both childhood and success, because his first life lesson on success came at the vulnerable age of seven, when he became the man of the house.

Elliot assumed that role after his father was killed breaking up an attempted robbery in a friend's store.

He is not great who is not greatly good.
—WILLIAM SHAKESPEARE

In the summer of 1992 the executive director of the Social Venture Network asked me if I knew Elliot Hoffman. She said that if there was one person who most exemplified what our group was about, it was this man.

Just Desserts, which is located in an enterprise zone, and its founder are renowned citizens of San Francisco. With community programs interwoven into the fabric of a $14 million-a-year business, Just Desserts has been cited by many, including national politicians, as a model workplace.

"If you could help us get Elliot to join our network," the director gushed, "I would be eternally grateful."

I did not know Elliot, but he was invited to be a guest at our next conference. He would be my roommate. He turned out to be nothing like I expected.

Driving up to an exclusive Santa Cruz, California, resort in a Honda, he told me: "Not much pickup, but the gas mileage is great." It was a small way to be mindful about how you live your life.

In many ways Elliot sticks out by not sticking out. He is a regular guy. Nice looking, he speaks in modulated tones, easy on the ear, yet with conviction. He listens more than he speaks and is easily agreeable—except when he disagrees. Yet even then he makes his point agreeably.

Elliot is what a politician should be, but he uses business, not politics, to achieve his desired ends.

We talked, we listened. At night our conversations were mostly about family, seldom about business or social activism. Elliot was concerned about spending time away from his family and his work—precious time.

Business was good, but he was in the planning stages of that twelve-month sabbatical, so he looked at every time decision through the lens of "Does this help me take the sabbatical?" We could not foresee that his family and business lives would not be the same after his leave. As he would later say, "From the year from heaven to the year from hell."

Out of a timber as crooked as that which man is made of, nothing perfectly straight can be carved.
—IMMANUEL KANT

Watching Elliot's postsabbatical years as a concerned bystander, I learned that he has his faults. He can be too paternalistic with his workers, too preoccupied with the community, too involved with the welfare of others—all at the expense of his business.

Shame on Elliot.

He can be stubborn. He cares so passionately about Just Desserts, about his family, about spaceship Earth, that at times he wears blinders.

Shame on Elliot.

He has trouble asking for help. His reputation in San Francisco is such that any notion that his business might need help would be met with . . .

Shame on Elliot.

In 1998, speaking to three hundred MBAs in Boston, I asked if anyone came from San Francisco. About fifteen people raised their hands.

Had they heard of Just Desserts? All had. One woman's comments could have been a company advertisement!

When I mentioned some financial troubles at the company, her response was total disbelief: "They are such a great place. Their cakes are fantastic, their cafés friendly. We all love going there. They hire all kinds of people.

"If they are having trouble, why don't they tell us? San Franciscans would all be glad to help out. Just tell us what to do, to buy, to give?"

Elliot's life tests our socially acceptable measures of success, our perceptions of what our values are in business and in life. He forces us to open up our hearts to ask again, "Am I a good person?"

His journey has taken him to the edge of the relationship

between money and values in our society, between what we say versus what we do and who we are versus who we hope to be.

What does it mean to be a good businessperson? Was Elliot a bad one, with his twenty-years of profit distributions for medical plans and paid leave? Does it matter that when he was recently hospitalized, he was showered with cards, flowers, and visits by most of his 320 employees? How do you weigh that fact against the knowledge that, when a bad quarter hit during his sabbatical, there was little in reserve?

Elliot's crime? When he made money, he gave it away to his workers and to the community. Then the rainy day came.

The most important human endeavor is the striving for morality in our actions. Our inner balance and even our very existence depends on it. Only morality in our actions can give beauty and dignity to life.
—ALBERT EINSTEIN

When I think of Elliot, I think of Jimmy Stewart as community banker George Bailey in Frank Capra's classic movie *It's a Wonderful Life*. George fought the greed in the world, tried to make his town a better place for all, and wondered if anyone even noticed. They did.

When his friends and neighbors heard he was in trouble because a forgetful uncle had misplaced a substantial sum of bank money, they showered him with support and cash.

On April 21, 1995, nine months after returning from his sabbatical to find his business in serious trouble, Elliot made a speech to the Social Venture Network, the same group that had wanted him to join so badly. He wondered aloud about our values, our relationship with money, what we truly care about, and what we would do.

It was one of the most moving, provocative speeches we

ever heard—a speech from the heart, an open letter to our community. Would we shower him with support and cash, too?

A hundred years from now it will not matter what my bank account was, the sort of house I lived in, or the kind of car I drove . . . but the world may be different because I was important in the life of a child.
—SIMONE WEIL

Elliot Hoffman was seven when his mother almost lost her will to live. Her lifelong sweetheart was dead, murdered at the age of thirty-one.

Murray Hoffman had gone out to get some talcum powder for his baby daughter. On the way, he dropped by a friend's clothing store in his Bronx neighborhood. He just wanted to say hello.

Instead he stopped a holdup at the store. He may even have saved the lives of the friend and his wife.

There was a shot. It was dark.

Elliot, who was playing at a neighbor's, was sent to an uncle's house along with his five-year-old brother, Neil, and five-month-old sister, Debbie. "Daddy is sick," Elliot was told. Elliot knew better. After a week he asked, "Is Daddy dead?"

Elliot's dad never made much money, even though he worked two jobs—milkman from two A.M. to six A.M., TV repairman from eight A.M. to six P.M. But "money was not a major issue, not a major focus of our life then nor of mine now," says Elliot.

"We didn't have much, but we weren't poor."

Family, friends, and community informed the values of Elliot's life. "To this day," he says, "old family friends tell me about my father and what a tremendous community person he was. Even though he had no money, when United Jewish

Appeal came around for a donation, he gave. When someone was in need, he was there.

"He gave time to people," says Elliot. "He gave of himself." And people in the neighborhood still talk about how much they miss Elliot's father. Perhaps no one more than this son.

"It had an impact on how I feel about my children and how I spend my time and my life," Elliot told me. "And I'd like to think that my own passion for community is a trait I inherited from him."

In the final analysis, it is not what you do for your children, but what you have taught them to do for themselves that will make them successful human beings.
—ANN LANDERS

At the time her husband was murdered in March 1955, Elliot's mother had never worked outside the home. For the sake of the children, she pulled herself together and got a job. They survived.

Their community and friends didn't stand back, either. With limited means, they collected $10,000 to help the Hoffman family.

Seven years after Elliot lost his father, his mother remarried. Being a stepson wasn't easy for Elliot. Although he admired his stepfather for taking on a family with three children, the fourteen-year-old Elliot and his mother's new husband were very different. Besides, the stepfather was too busy running his own prospering business to share in many of Elliot's interests.

The family moved to Long Island, and a few years later Elliot happily went off to college. He spent two years at Ohio University and then returned to New York to finish his education at New York University. Hanging out in Greenwich Village, he sported the requisite beard and ponytail.

The moral flabbiness born of the exclusive worship of the bitch-goddess SUCCESS. That, with the squalid cash interpretation of "success," is our national disease.
—WILLIAM JAMES

It was the end of the 1960s, a time of restless energy. The generation that grew up listening to the Beatles and *Sgt. Pepper* was heading out into the world, searching for truth, trying to find themselves—and having fun doing it. The Vietnam antiwar movement was at its peak.

For Elliot, it was "a great, huge experience, especially for someone from the other side of the tracks. . . . I was questioning all the values I had been handed as a kid and opening my mind to alternative ways of thinking and being."

At NYU, the aforementioned course requirement at Manufacturers Hanover Trust opened Elliot's eyes to a world that measured value and conferred meaning on the moment-to-moment movement of stock prices. Despite his dismay, Elliot dutifully embarked on a well-trodden corporate path after graduation.

He was recruited for RCA's computer business, one of a thousand new hires, and hustled off to a campus in New Jersey for ten weeks of training. Of the thousand new hires, only he wore a beard.

In May 1970 the Vietnam War came to Ohio's Kent State University, when National Guardsmen broke up a nonviolent antiwar protest by shooting eight students, killing four. Elliot recalls being the only member of his RCA training squad who responded with anger and sadness.

"I felt I had no community for my feelings," he says.

Training completed, he was assigned to the New York office to analyze systems flows, what he calls "meaningless drivel." Soon thereafter his supervisor announced, "Either the beard goes or you go." That made it easy.

"It was one of the most memorable days of my life," he

muses joyfully. "I was free of the shackles. I knew that from that point on, I would not do something that I didn't feel good about, that did not connect with me soulfully, that did not connect with my passion or my values."

Elliot would never again leave his real self behind or go where he could not recognize himself. He set out to be a certain kind of person and to lead a certain kind of life, one that he himself would shape and color.

Through a series of odd jobs, friends, and coincidences, Elliot found his way to San Francisco. In March 1971 he decided that city would be his new home.

The goal is not to have but to be, not to own but to give, not to control but to share, not to subdue but to be in accord . . . not to amass, but to face sacred moments.
—ABRAHAM HESCHEL

He soon met his soul mate, a speech therapist named Gail Horvath. Gail was the only woman in a mountain-climbing class in the Eldorado National Forest. "We fell in love over the campfire," Elliot says.

In September 1973, at a party for Gail's twenty-fourth birthday, Just Desserts was born. Elliot baked the birthday cake, using a borrowed recipe for cheesecake. His confection was an immediate hit.

One couple at the party were about to open a café. They liked the cheesecake so much that they urged Elliot to supply it. "We had actually been toying with the idea of starting our own business," Elliot recalls, "so we said we'd give it a try."

Gail and Elliot started baking cheesecakes in their apartment. "We would deliver them to the café every day," Elliot explains. "The response was incredible. People went crazy."

The first person Elliot hired was the woman who had given him the cheesecake recipe.

For the next twenty years—until his sabbatical—Just Desserts blossomed into a much storied business success: more and more restaurant customers for Elliot and Gail, cafés of their own, friend after friend helping with recipes, deliveries, and new store locations.

A newspaper article sparked more sales. Then came radio interviews, television profiles, news stories, and several awards for product quality and community involvement. Elliot, Gail, and Just Desserts were the darlings of San Francisco and, admits Elliot, "it just blew our minds."

"We enjoyed this early business success because we were both dedicated and stupid," he recalls.

"We had no clue to what we were doing. We baked everything with real butter, real eggs—all real ingredients. At the time, nobody else was doing that. Baking in this country emphasized cheap ingredients to keep costs down so you could make a lot of money, but our attitude was that we were making great stuff for friends who were coming over for dessert.

"We're in the business of creating wonderful treats for people—treats for the world. And we want to make them great. Our product is a celebratory kind of thing, something special. It always brings a smile," Elliot goes on.

"It's a good feeling to help people feel good. Maybe that comes from my father. But when I can make someone feel good and smile, I feel great. I want to help change the world by making it a little happier place."

I arise in the morning torn between the desire to improve the world and a desire to enjoy the world. This makes it hard to plan the day.
—E. B. White

Early growth was slowed because "profit was a four-letter word," says Elliot. "It took me five or six years before I understood that what really counts is how you make a profit and what you do with it."

That understanding helped Elliot focus on increased profitability, leading to more community involvement, and the foundation of a model workplace. "You can do well by doing good, and I say bullshit to the person who doesn't think so," declares Elliot.

In 1984 Elliot articulated a three-part vision for Just Desserts: to be recognized as one of the finest bakeries in the world, to be recognized as a model workplace and a participating member of the community, and to make a healthy profit. The company did all three.

On the first anniversary of the business, Elliot and Gail threw a party for the community—champagne and a huge cake, of course, for thousands of people.

After all, "it was the community that was making us successful," Elliot explains. "It seemed the natural thing to do."

**A business that makes nothing but money
is a poor kind of business.**
—HENRY FORD

In the 1980s Elliot became increasingly involved in community work. He began serving on various committees, dealing with matters ranging from conditions in the state prison to the city's rent-control system.

His renowned Garden Project began in 1990. Working with parolees, Elliot turned the garbage-strewn half-acre plot next to the bakery into an elaborate organic garden, where parolees learn the skills of gardening "to heal their environment, their communities, and ultimately themselves."

Just Desserts received regular visits from local to presidential politicians, each one commenting on its commitment to diversity.

"From the get-go, we tried to harness the power of diversity—men and women, diverse ethnic backgrounds, many languages—and you can see the difference in the quality of our product and the success of our enterprise.

"You could have the same building right across the street, with the same ovens and equipment, the same recipes and same ingredients, and I'll guarantee that your chocolate cake would taste different. The caring and love our employees put into the product is a reflection of the caring and love they feel from Just Desserts," proudly states Elliot in the book *Leading People,* which honored him for his diverse workforce.

> **They may forget what you said, but they will never forget how you made them feel.**
> —CARL BUEHNER

For twenty years Just Desserts made money every quarter. Always. But when there could have been a profit of 8 percent a year, 9 percent, even 10 percent, its best year saw a 3.5 percent pretax profit.

There was a reason for that: Elliot Hoffman measured profits as more than just money. More could always be squeezed from annual earnings, but Elliot preferred to allocate those resources to the workplace, the workers, the community, and business improvements.

Of course, if you measure profit as Elliot does—what Just Desserts gives to all its stakeholders—then profitability is off the charts.

"The whole thing," he says, "was a feeling of being in tune with what is right for me. If someone else wants to do the corporate thing, more power to them. But it wasn't for me. This was. This is."

At a time when such issues were not even part of the national debate, Just Desserts was building a business on its founders' values. Did Elliot and Gail feel out of sync? Only with what was going on around them. They felt entirely in sync with their own core values, with their own units of measurement—and with each other.

> **Imagine life as a game in which you are juggling**
> **five balls . . . work, family, health, friends, and spirit.**
> **Work is a rubber ball. If you drop it, it will bounce back.**
> **But the other four balls are made of glass.**
> **If you drop one of these, they will never be the same.**
> —BRIAN DYSON

After living together for five years, Gail and Elliot married in 1979. Miles was born in 1980, after which Gail took off two years. Joanna was born in 1986, after which Gail took off eight years. The bakery was not her journey; it was Elliot's.

Between the business and his community involvement, Elliot always made time for family. But in his own eyes, it still wasn't enough. He decided that when Miles was thirteen years old, he'd take a year off. He didn't want to be one of those fathers who realized too late that his kids were grown and gone and that he had missed it.

A year for himself and his family—that was something worth working for. From 1988 until 1993 the commitment to the sabbatical became the key filter through which Elliot sifted many of his decisions.

The company was healthy, and by 1993 profits were stable. He spent the last year strengthening the management team, bringing in a good chief operating officer.

**I wish that I had known sooner that if you miss a child's
play or performance or sporting event, you will have
forgotten a year later the work emergency that caused
you to miss it. But the child won't have forgotten
that you weren't there.**
—LAUREL CUTLER

The sabbatical year was idyllic, "the best year of my life,"
Elliot recalls wistfully. There was a three-month, around-
the-world family trip; a father-son trip to Alaska; a father-
daughter trip to Disney World.

It was Elliot who took the kids to school and picked them
up. He swam, he read, he went on walks with Gail. He spent
"one year living life."

It changed his perspective, gave him a better sense of balance "in the proverbial struggle between family and business
and community." It confirmed for him what counted—and
what didn't.

Elliot's friends envied his time off. He even persuaded two
billionaires to consider taking sabbaticals for themselves. But
when all was said and done, Elliot was the person who actually did it.

"It turned out that it was always a bad time for either of
them to take off," he explained. "Maybe another year."

**There are people who have money
and people who are rich.**
—COCO CHANEL

When Elliot returned from his sabbatical, Just Desserts was
in the midst of its worst year ever. The marketplace had
changed, there was strong new competition, and retail sales

had begun to slide. Elliot's own mistakes had come home to roost, and reserves were low.

Elliot's shortsightedness had painful consequences, including the dismissal of a number of workers who were not just colleagues, but close friends. The bakery's first employee, Elliot and Gail's friend with the cheesecake recipe, was a casualty. It took five years before she and Elliot could begin the healing process.

"It was devastating," admits Elliot. "I had done this blissful sabbatical, something that society says you're not allowed to do, and it was as if the universe were saying 'Screw you.'" What's more, investors saw Elliot's sabbatical as a signal that he wasn't serious about Just Desserts. From 1994 to 1997 the message was that he was failing.

But Elliot didn't think so. Oh, he had some bad moments: night sweats worrying about how to pay for the kids' education, the mortgage, the "what will people say" question. But deep down he knew his kids would be fine, that he and Gail would manage, and that it didn't really matter what people said.

The "greed and growth" majority might measure him a failure, but Elliot Hoffman didn't agree.

> **Possessing material comforts in no way guarantees happiness. Only spiritual wealth can bring true happiness. If that is correct, should business be concerned only with the material aspect of life and leave the care of the human spirit to religion?**
> —KONOSUKE MATSUSHITA

Elliot dug in. He made a journey into the capital markets in search of investors, then backed right out. He made his moving speech to the Social Venture Network. He got a standing ovation, some hugs, a little help, but mostly emotional support. Money and values don't always mix.

He realized soon thereafter that most venture capital isn't partial to his brand of business. "The way capital works is not the world I play in. It's a world in which the only criterion is return on investment. Cash taken out for cash put in.

"To venture capitalists, the Garden Project, for example, is a 'nice touch,' window dressing, clever promotion. Never mind that ex-prisoners have sown productive lives in the Garden instead of dealing drugs, robbing someone you know, or serving time in another prison. Don't we all reap the fruits of that kind of success?

"Must money be the sole concern? What about concern for the soul? ROI—return on investment—is easy. What about ROC, return on community, or ROH, return on humanity? Isn't the real bottom line a multiple return that puts human and social rewards alongside financial rewards?" Elliot asks eloquently.

He soon realized that he and his colleagues at Just Desserts would have to bail themselves out. "I said to the management team to forget the idea of raising money. Put it away. It's not going to happen until we turn ourselves around. It's totally up to us. We have to focus only on what we need to do to make Just Desserts profitable again."

**A man is rich in proportion to
the things he can afford to let alone.**
—HENRY DAVID THOREAU

Reinvigorated, Elliot returned to being a hands-on business manager. But he continued to maintain a balance between business and home.

"There's no doubt in my mind that if I spent eighteen hours a day with the business and none with my family and none with the community, the business would be worse off. If you don't lead some semblance of a balanced life, you are going to make poor decisions in all parts of your life. This is common sense to me."

Energized by the emotional support of Gail and friends, he has had energy to spare. Focused, he found that things began to align. Within three years Just Desserts was financially solvent again. After five the company's health returned. Gail has now been able to go back to her own pursuits, which means more time for family and her work in hospices.

The turnaround did not come at the expense of the human side of the ledger. Elliot did not toss aside his commitment to a happy workplace or forgo the company's community involvement to buy black ink for today's balance sheet. But he had to make personal adjustments—at least for the time being.

Success means living the life of the heart.
—FRANCIS FORD COPPOLA

"I've had to take chunks of time, say, in six-month blocks, and dedicate that to the business," admits Elliot. "I have eased up on my outside community endeavors for the time being. It is a necessary rebalancing that is ultimately rewarding to me, my family, and all our loyal people at Just Desserts."

Elliot and his new management team have shifted the company's focus to the wholesale market. Sales are booming, but there is still work to be done internally if Just Desserts is to remain that model workplace. "We had lost some of our spirit and inadvertently grown into a less diverse company," Elliot admits. "Our team is now helping to bring us back to what we want to be as a company."

Elliot is proving there doesn't have to be "a disconnect between our relationship with money and our espoused values. Money is a resource to be used to improve the quality of life on earth and in our communities, to provide hope for a decent future."

"We are not really searching for money," Elliot says. "We are looking for a quality of life having very little to do with material wealth. We are all desperately searching for intimacy—with each other, with ourselves, with the natural world. We can do that in our own ways by making the world a touch better."

> **Money's easy to make if it's money you want.**
> **But with few exceptions, people don't want money.**
> **They want . . . love and admiration.**
> —JOHN STEINBECK

✳

Lifelines

Is it worth it to work hard to send your children to private schools and colleges if the price is not getting to know your children before they go away from home?

There is an ancient Polynesian expression that says, "We are standing on whales, fishing for minnows." Though definitions of success come in many shapes and sizes, often the most important are right in front of us. Yet we may fail to see them, especially when it seems the entire world dictates what those measurements, our values, should be.

We are looking for measures of success beyond the material—measures that fit with who we want to be and how we choose to spend our lives. It is important to develop a personal definition of success, one meant not to impress others, but to express ourselves.

What inspires you to feel good about yourself, to feel you are a good human being?

For Elliot Hoffman, success included family, friends, and community—the life of the heart. It meant integrating these needs into a profitable, humanistic workplace that honored the meaning of "businessperson." It meant that at times he had to pay the price for his values. But in time it was those values that made his life meaningful and brought his business back to profitability.

We are prone to judge success by the index of our salaries or the size of our automobiles rather than by the quality of our service and relationship to mankind.
—DR. MARTIN LUTHER KING JR.

CHAPTER 5

✳

BRING YOUR VALUES TO WORK

Ira Jackson's Capitalism

————————

The work praises the man.
—IRISH PROVERB

**The brain is a wonderful organ; it starts working
the moment you get up in the morning,
and does not stop until you get into the office.**
—ROBERT FROST

I was getting a paycheck, but not a psychic paycheck. I want to do something that is valuable and needed. I want to give back."

This lament—from one of the students in my seminar at Simmons Business School in Boston—is one I hear regularly from students and managers everywhere.

It's one thing to be an entrepreneur, like Elliot Hoffman, but what about the rest of us who pursue careers in the corporate world? It's not so easy to bring your personal values into most corporate cultures.

Before the Industrial Revolution, when economies were agriculturally based, people worked where they lived and entire families were usually employed in the same business. It was much easier to bring your values to work.

More than 80 percent of the world's business is still family business, but situations today are different. Most of us neither work on a farm nor live above the family store. Work and family are often two separate lives—and, for many, separate value systems as well.

Although charity may indeed begin at home, far too often it stays hidden there, like some family embarrassment. As a child, I remember grown-ups saying things such as "So and so is a great businessman. He's tough. He knows how to get what he wants. He can outnegotiate anybody. He could even sell a refrigerator to an Alaskan!"

If questions were raised about values, the response was: "But that's business. He would never act that way at home. That's different."

The notion that it is normal to behave one way in business and virtually the opposite way at home has become ingrained in our culture. It is a recipe for confusion, perhaps especially for working women, who sometimes feel disliked by their colleagues if they act tough, and discounted if they don't.

It seems that we have one head that is expected to wear two totally different hats—one at home, the other at work. Some of our toughest colleagues have seemingly developed two hearts as well, separating their emotions into business values and personal values. As they see it, business can't possibly be personal.

But can life be fun and fulfilling with half a soul?

Is my work smaller than my soul?
—MATTHEW FOX

Not surprisingly, a number of people are troubled by this artificial dichotomy. According to a *USA Today* survey, more than 46 percent of Americans admit to unethical behavior on the job and say they would never do such things at home. And what are we to make of the fact that more people commit suicide at nine o'clock Monday morning than on any other day or time of the week?

For thousands of middle managers, spiritual turmoil is all too frequent. It shows how much we care and how conflicted we are between making a living at a job we need in order to support our families and making a life with the values we know we need to really live.

Most people crave the pleasure of doing honest work for a good purpose that reflects their personal values. Our own survey results of MBA students and graduates five to fifteen years out speak strongly to this issue:

- More than half of the 2,300 respondents we surveyed in 1996 at fifty top business schools were willing to take a 10 percent or greater salary reduction to work at a company that had values consistent with their own.
- When second-year students were asked to choose among ten criteria for job selection, the overall choice was "values that are similar to mine" (number one with women; number two with men after financial compensation).
- After graduation, women wanted to ensure they had meaningful work. Men sought learning and financial rewards. Ten years later women were looking for balance and fulfillment outside work (translation: time with family), whereas the men now badly wanted meaningful work.

**Where the spirit does not work with the hand,
there is no art.**
—LEONARDO DA VINCI

The preachers among us urge that we get our values in order and apply them equally to both sides of our lives. Stay true to yourself at all times, in all seasons, they say. But integrity— that unwillingness, as Erich Fromm wrote, to violate one's own identity—is easier prescribed than achieved in the real world.

Most of the people profiled in this book have tried to be company players at one point or another but found themselves in conflict with their own values. They started their own businesses, believing that independence would allow them to be true to themselves. The reality, though, is that running your own business provides no assurance that all your values will survive bottom-line pressures or even stay alive in the very business you designed for them.

Success eliminates as many options as does failure.
—M. SCOTT PECK

At a conference in 1990 I was speaking from the dais and well into my warmest inspirational mode when Ben Cohen (of Ben & Jerry's ice cream fame) handed me a dose of my own medicine. "Come on, Marco," he heckled, "let's see you try to make your values work in a business."

It was a challenge that I had to accept or risk being seen as full of hot air.

Soon thereafter I persuaded a childhood friend, Paul Birn-holz, to join me in launching a Vermont pet products company named Applebrook Farms, Inc. It was an opportunity to instill my values from the ground up—and in concert with a friend whose values were the same as mine, if not stronger.

Circumstances of the business, which was started as a sideline, a hobby of sorts, allowed us to take the time to do things right. But even that luxury, combined with increasing financial success, was no guarantee that we could actually align our values with the company's business reality.

Part of our mission was to increase employment in Vermont. But when a potentially large shift in demand arose, we had to look at moving production to the Midwest in order to lower costs. The result would be more machinery and fewer people. It even meant that our "Moon Over Vermont" moon-shaped dog biscuits could no longer be moon shaped.

When we experimented with giving 10 percent of product revenues to fund community service scholarships in a Vermont school, customers in Connecticut were upset. Why should they pay to support education in Vermont when Connecticut had its own educational issues?

When we tried to employ homeless people in the basement of a church, the government required full supervision and full workers' compensation for individuals who would commonly work less than ten hours per week. Cost? Prohibitive.

And when we had the potential to increase the size of the company rapidly in six months, neither Paul nor I wanted to run it. It was becoming too much of a business and not as much fun as when it was just a hobby. (One of our unexpressed purposes of the company was "to give us more opportunities to spend time together and have fun.")

Of course, it can be even more difficult when you try to inject your personal values into a large, already operating company, the very belly of the proverbial beast. Which brings me to Ira Jackson and why I admire him so much.

> **No one can serve two masters;**
> **for either he will hate the one and love the other,**
> **or he will hold to one and despise the other.**
> —LUKE 16:13

There is an old Groucho Marx joke about a guy who goes to a psychiatrist. He says that he doesn't have a problem, but, rather, it is his brother who has the problem. The brother thinks he is a chicken.

The psychiatrist responds: "Why not just tell him he isn't a chicken and be done with it?" To which the man counters, "I would like to, but we need the eggs."

Ira Jackson is a man who viewed his life as a labor of love in the public sector. He expressed his passion for social and economic justice in a range of jobs in both government and academia. But when faced with the reality of trying to send four children to college on a public sector paycheck, Ira decided he needed the eggs.

But could he, with his background and experience and values, feel at home in a commercial bank—the den of capitalism—where the values were surely far different?

"I took a thirty-five-thousand-foot look at the idea," recalls Ira. "And it looked different. My friends thought I was crazy. I saw only a challenge, an opportunity, with great potential rewards and impact. The bank seemed sincere. And if it didn't work out, I could always find a job back in the public sector."

From thirty-five thousand feet, his ambivalence had taken on a different hue. It was still BankBoston Corporation, the Harvard of the financial industry, the oldest commercial bank in the United States, an institution with an important history—and, admittedly, the private sector was uncharted territory for Ira Jackson. But therein lay the attraction.

"I can do this," he decided. "I can add value."

His confidence wilted the first day on the job. He got on the elevator and looked around at a sea of starched white shirts on starched-looking white men. This was not what he was used to.

Doubts arose. The proverbial knot in the stomach appeared. Ira accused himself of having sold out: "What am I doing at a bank?" But therein began a quest common to many of us: the attempt to marry not-for-profit values with a for-profit paycheck.

Opportunities are seldom labeled.
—WILLIAM FEATHER

Long ago and far away, in some perhaps mythical era of commercial history, banking was known as a largely community service business. Most banks still profess, if not stress, this aspect of their business, and many retain community-focused divisions.

But community service is distinctly not central to a bank's assets or interests today. Trying to make it so is no way to build a banking career, much less acquire a corner office—unless you are Ira Jackson.

Ira is an executive vice president at BankBoston, a major New England lender. He was instrumental in transforming the bank into an institution highly regarded for community service and social concern. He also found a way to make his values work at work—even with the demands of a public financial institution and a visible, high-ranking job serving as daily reminders of fiduciary responsibilities.

> **You can't push a wave onto the shore**
> **any faster than the ocean brings it in.**
> —SUSAN STRASBERG

I first met Ira in the fall of 1989, when he was about a year into his new job at BankBoston. He was forty-one years old, and I knew that he had already served as an aide to two of the country's most interesting inner-city leaders, as an administrator at the Kennedy School, and as commissioner of revenue in Massachusetts.

I was trying to finance a multimedia project linking businesses with social issue courses taught in Massachusetts public schools. A good friend, Dan Small, introduced Ira to me as a kindred spirit who might be interested in helping the project.

Ira was in charge of the bank's external affairs, focused on corporate philanthropy. He wasn't satisfied that most of BankBoston's patronage was dutiful, unimaginative, and not particularly effective. He hoped to inject more creativity, reinforced by a 10 percent hike in the bank's philanthropy budget.

We met twice. He found my project intriguing but felt he could free up only about $50,000. Project fees started at $500,000, and I knew that I could not give him any real value for his $50,000. So I politely refused, although I appreciated that he was willing to offer some serious money, mostly on the basis of a friend's referral.

Then Ira gave me a gift greater than money. He referred me to Geralyn White, a friend from his days at Harvard University's Kennedy School of Government. In time Geralyn introduced me to many socially responsible entrepreneurs through the Social Venture Network.

As I was leaving Ira that day, I asked him how long someone with his background and soul could stay at a bank. How could a person so committed to social justice find satisfaction in a for-profit institution? How could he bring that passion into alignment with the goals of a bank? What would be his challenges, his compromises?

> **The size of your success
> is determined by the size of your belief.**
> —LUCIUS ANNAEUS SENECA

Ira Jackson forged his early work life out of the wisdom he received from his parents' New Deal generation. They believed that the public sector was the only place for people committed to social and political change.

Ira was born in 1948 into a family of liberal Jewish Democrats. His grandparents were Russian immigrants; one of his parents was a teacher, the other a lawyer. He attended Adlai Stevenson's campaign rallies at the age of four and later watched his mother go off to Washington, D.C., for the great civil rights march of 1963.

As a Harvard undergraduate, Ira explored careers that matched his ideals. He worked to build affordable housing in Boston and pursued Democratic Party politics. A committed Jew, he also tried to follow the central Talmudic teaching to "make the world a better place . . . to not turn away from one in need, and remember the stranger, as we were once strangers ourselves."

After graduation, though, Ira initially floundered in his quest for a job that matched his ideals. One of several dead ends involved working in California as a talent coordinator for Joey Bishop's television show. Social justice wasn't on Joey's program.

Drifting back to the East, Ira signed on as a junior instructor at Essex Community College in Newark, New Jersey. At the same time he worked toward a graduate degree in urban planning at Rutgers University. Fate was about to hand him his future.

Events shape values, as much as values shape events.
—CHARLES HANDY

It was the height of the 1970s urban riots. While driving through Newark one tense night, Ira, perhaps the only white person in that neighborhood, spotted a car with a Harvard decal on the rear window. He waved at the driver and, before long, found himself chatting at the side of the road.

The driver turned out to be the father of one of his Harvard classmates. And not only that, he was also the president of the Newark Board of Education.

"Get yourself a shave," he ordered Ira. "Put on a tie and a jacket, and see me tomorrow morning in my office."

When Ira arrived the next day, someone else was in the office, too. It was Kenneth Gibson, the newly elected mayor of Newark. Without hesitation Gibson came to the point.

"Ira, would you like to come work for me?"

"Mr. Mayor," Ira said, "I don't know anything about city government."

"Neither do I. We'll learn together."

Ken Gibson was the first black elected mayor of a major city in the Northeast. Expectations were high. The work was challenging, exciting, full of opportunities for social change. Ira's influence rose with his hard work and his good political instincts.

Not much time for an outside life, but he didn't care. Not much money, but he didn't care. Ira Jackson was fully committed. Sometimes it seemed he was working twenty-four hours a day, seven days a week, but "I was putting to work all the skills I had and developing new ones. And Ken was like a father to me."

Ira improvised as he went along, learning from mistakes. Eventually he served as Gibson's chief of staff and liaison with the White House—positions in which he had the mayor's ear, positions in which he could influence policies that would influence lives, positions that also exposed him to an extraordinary set of contacts.

One was Kevin White, mayor of Boston. "If you ever want to come home," White told Ira, "you've got a job with me."

After several years away, coming back to Boston seemed like a good idea. Ira went to work for White, serving as his chief aide throughout the difficult period of Boston's school busing struggle.

It was an era that challenged Ira's assumptions about social justice and the role of government. He reaffirmed some deep-seated values, modified others. He learned about compromise and about being practical. He studied the ins and outs of real-life politics with a master.

In fact, Mayor Kevin White, who was like a father to Ira, would soon become an actual relative: his niece Martha became Ira's wife.

**It's not hard to make decisions
when you know what your values are.**
—ROY DISNEY

Ira was increasingly interested in a larger forum, a place he could learn more about national and global social issues. He loved the cities of Gibson and White, but he was ready to expand his horizons.

The opportunity came when the Kennedy School set out to develop a program for newly elected big-city mayors. Launching the program ended Ira's political activism, but the new role seemed to fit him and his new family. He could even pick up a graduate degree at the same time.

One of his teachers was Graham Allison, a government professor with considerable experience as a Pentagon official. Harvard's president, Derek Bok, had tapped Allison to become dean of the Kennedy School with the challenge to transform the school into a powerhouse, an equal of the university's law, medical, and business schools.

Dean Allison chose Ira Jackson as his second in command. Ira spent seven years as his junior officer on deck—years that Ira describes as "highly entrepreneurial, fun, completely out of the box." Although he was still number two, Ira had the opportunity to test his values in an entirely different venue: the cosmopolitan world of Harvard, with its global reach to all kinds of ideas, minds, cultures, and power structures.

"Of all we accomplished," Ira states, "I'm proudest of the forum space—a transformational space that helped give expression to what the school was trying to be, a place where the commerce of democracy was taking place."

In Ira's mind, his work at the Kennedy School was a prime example of making a difference by living his values. But how much was he really doing? Action was limited, though he felt he was clearly helping others to make government and politics a little better.

> **Wisdom is knowing what to do next, skill is knowing how to do it, and virtue is doing it.**
> —DAVID STARR JORDAN

One of Jackson's Brookline, Massachusetts, neighbors was Michael Dukakis. Ira even baby-sat for the Dukakis children. When Dukakis became governor, he asked the now high-profile Ira Jackson to serve as state commissioner of revenue and to clean up a department reeling from charges of corruption.

"Why would you become a tax collector?" Ira's incredulous friends asked. "There's no glory in the job, no visibility, no creativity. It's just a big factory."

Little did they know that Ira had always wanted to "see if I could make a difference in the efficiency of an organization, like making trains go faster or the tax refunds go out more honestly." The job would also give him the opportunity to be first in command. For the first time it would be up to Ira, no one else.

He accepted the governor's offer. Where else but as the tax commissioner could he more directly affect issues of social justice?

> **I am sustained by knowing that I am doing what is right.**
> —ARCHBISHOP DESMOND TUTU

The challenges were huge. Public confidence was at rock bottom. The department's integrity and morale were both depleted. Ira felt that "my only choice was to impose discipline and make the department work more efficiently. I didn't make a lot of friends."

When Ira Jackson decides to move ahead, other people find themselves moving ineluctably in the same direction. His message soon becomes clear: "If it's on my agenda, I hope it's on yours, too."

Ira remembers thinking, We've got to run this like a business. It is a business, the people's business—the people of our commonwealth. And Dukakis had given him the freedom to manage that business as he saw best. But would the people of Massachusetts, to say nothing of his fellow tax collectors, approve Commissioner Jackson's management style?

When in doubt, tell the truth. You will gratify some of the people and astound the rest.
—MARK TWAIN

Ira pledged that tax refunds would be sent within one month of taxpayers' filing error-free returns, compared with a previous minimum of four months. But thanks to what he praised as the "extraordinary commitment of a large number of our four thousand employees," the refunds actually went out in just eleven days.

That feat went a long way toward restoring public confidence—and exhausted a lot of state employees.

But ensuring social justice for the taxpaying public was only part of the task. Another constituency, a staff of four thousand, was equally important. Ira knew them: they were his grandparents, his high school classmates, the people who perhaps had not gone on to college—"poorly served, unfairly treated."

So Ira made it his business in his five years as revenue commissioner to "deliver not only the results that the public deserved, but also the results that at least four thousand employees always should have had, which was good leadership and sound management—and lots of support."

There are few more direct ways of working for social justice than being responsible for the livelihoods of four thousand people and responsible to a statewide population of six million. Ira became well-known and widely applauded for his performance in bringing both courtesy and efficiency to tax collecting in Massachusetts. The 1980s were also a boom time for the commonwealth, which made his job easier. Why would he leave?

Ira had worked hard. He had four children. He also had a $60,000 salary with no outside income permitted in a state with a high cost of living—and with $30,000 college tuitions looming on the horizon.

Ira's jobs had always accommodated and reinforced his values. But what happens if you work in an organization where the public interest is not the first thing on everybody's mind or even the last? And how do you make that transition into the private sector?

Ira would soon find out. Invited to a meeting at Bank-Boston, he was offered a job that posed a challenge unlike any he had even considered before. It was a fundamental test of his values in a world presumably alien to those values.

> **If I am not for myself, who is for me? If I am
> only for myself, what am I? And if not now, when?**
> —HILLEL

"This is an institution that needs to change," Ira Stepanian, then BankBoston's chief executive, informed Ira. "We don't even know how it needs to change, but we want to put you in charge of external affairs [today called corporate and community affairs] and give you the freedom and flexibility to do what you think appropriate. Your portfolio includes communications, media, philanthropy, and government relations. And you'll be a member of the executive committee. What do you say?"

It was quite an offer, but as the state revenue commissioner well knew, BankBoston had problems—lots of them. Not the least of which was that, a couple of years earlier, the bank had been accused of laundering money and violating currency-transaction reporting. It was a front-page story, the bank paid a stiff fine, and its management was hugely embarrassed.

What's more, where he was number one, the go-to guy, as revenue commissioner, here he would be only a player on the team, not the captain.

As for working in the private sector—in a bank, of all places—it had never been part of Ira Jackson's game plan. And after nearly two decades of fulfilling public service work, he knew what kind of work he was raised to do—or thought he knew.

True, the money was good, and that wasn't a trivial issue. But even though Ira felt financially pinched from a career in public service, money was never his goal. Moreover, he assumed that a culture of greed ruled commercial banks, and greed was the enemy he had always fought. How could he join them?

But then Ira took his thirty-five-thousand-foot look and, against the wishes of friends, figured he had nothing to lose. He assumed he would simply be a fish out of water, gasping for air. What he did not foresee was the bank's reaction: as Ira's hard work and effectiveness boosted his credibility, BankBoston became an increasingly friendly accomplice. His work would even be praised.

He who would learn to fly must first learn to walk and run and climb and dance; one cannot fly into flying.
—FRIEDRICH WILHELM NIETZSCHE

Throughout his dozen years at BankBoston, little by little, one step at a time, Ira brought his values to bear—carefully, skillfully, like a master politician. He knew when to push and when to step back. He knew when to build a public constituency and when to keep things private. He knew how to focus patiently on one issue at a time.

Value conflicts arose at times, but as his efforts paid off, his concerns received serious consideration from the other members of the executive committee. Ira did his part by working to ensure that his concerns were aligned with the bank's best interests, and then he pushed to be more creative about how that played out.

The hours were long. It was a struggle to find time for Martha and his four children, what with the endless nights of charity dinners and fund-raisers. But "at least the nights were spent with organizations whose missions I believed in—causes I was proud to support and proud that my company was involved in, too."

He remained staunch in his support of Jewish organizations, including the New England Holocaust Memorial, where he championed the cause of corporate philanthropy and support. When bank investments touched on social issues, Ira raised his concerns. His sentiments were honored.

Ira learned that "not everybody in the private sector is driven by greed." What's more, he began to see a unique opportunity at the bank. Just as he had been entrepreneurial and businesslike in the public sector, he now saw a chance to bring a public perspective to the private sector. In fact, "the opportunity for change was so vast," Ira notes, "that even the smallest action could alter direction and cast off the winds of change."

**Always be a first-rate version of yourself,
instead of a second-rate version of somebody else.**
—JUDY GARLAND

Ira has launched all sorts of programs that do credit to Bank-Boston, starting with City Year, the program he began just after arriving at the bank. The idea was to bring young people together in multiracial, socially diverse teams for a year of work to improve the infrastructure of urban neighborhoods. At year's end participants get college scholarships matching the stipends they earned working together.

Ira committed BankBoston to provide the seed money for City Year, which by 1998 spanned eight cities from Boston to Los Angeles and had received numerous awards from corporations as well as public interest groups and President Clinton.

City Year was Ira's first step toward redefining Bank-Boston's philanthropic role, from vicarious contributor to social venture capitalist. Ira also helped redefine the breadth of the bank's giving. Money, he believed, was just one of the currencies available to BankBoston. A lot of talent and expertise resided in its people. Why couldn't Bank-Boston contribute that currency? Why couldn't employees be philanthropists, too—in time as well as money?

Ira committed BankBoston to a program called "Success by Six," which was aimed at galvanizing public resources and attention to make kids learning-ready by the age of six—"a prevention and investment strategy," Ira calls it, and "a new departure for corporate giving."

The commitment didn't just call for dollars, it involved "bringing together several disciplines, constituencies, and governmental bodies," Ira recounts. "Bank personnel went on site visits, we used best-practices assessments, we articulated public policy issues, and we even did some legislative lobbying, along with the new allies we made with leaders from organized labor, the academy, and the community—unusual for a commercial bank."

All this unbankerlike behavior was supported and spearheaded by BankBoston senior management, especially Chief Executive Officer Chad Gifford. It is the same Chad Gifford who has only one picture on his office wall: it shows Aaron Feuerstein, president of the famously humane textile firm Malden Mills. After Feuerstein's mills burned down in December 1995, it was BankBoston that arranged some very creative financing to keep Feuerstein's dream alive by rebuilding the mills.

It is the same Chad Gifford who has consistently supported the development of the Community Banking Group (CBG), BankBoston's "urban investment bank."

With $2 billion in deposits at fifty urban branches, the CBG is, as *Fortune* magazine labeled it, "the most ambitious and radical urban banking initiative in the country." Run by highly respected, thirty-year BankBoston veteran Gail Snowden, CBG now maintains a healthy return of equity and pursues what Ira describes as "capitalism with a conscience . . . in effect doing well by doing good."

> **There may be times when we are powerless
> to prevent injustice, but there must never be
> a time when we fail to protest.**
> —ELIE WIESEL

Ira's office on the twenty-fifth floor of BankBoston's Federal Street headquarters has been the source of a range of initiatives that have made a difference—from sponsorship of cultural events to community banking to investing in social entrepreneurs. But much of this work has also been directed to what goes on inside the bank.

For example, when senior management announced that two thousand employees would have to be laid off, the external affairs department went to work with a vengeance to mitigate the impact.

Spurred by a question from Bernard Cardinal Law, head of Boston's Roman Catholic diocese—who asked, "Why must capitalism operate with so little conscience?"—Ira sought assistance from the then U.S. secretary of labor, Robert Reich, and from Harvard Business School professor Rosabeth Moss Kanter. He then approached the bank's human resources department, helping them to shape a model transition assistance program. Together they worked out a plan that reduced the two thousand layoffs to five hundred.

How? Through good management. "Almost nobody in the private sector manages attrition or makes the tough decisions to minimize the pain," says Ira. "BankBoston did."

For the five hundred pink-slipped workers, the bank offered generous severance, personalized career counseling and financial planning, $2,500 in tuition for retraining, and a range of options for assistance in starting a business, working for the nonprofit sector, even incentives for working elsewhere in the financial industry.

It is a program that made an enormous difference to the 500 former BankBoston employees. It also made an enormous difference to the 23,500 remaining BankBoston employees.

Work is love made visible.
—KAHLIL GIBRAN

Commitment. The single most important ingredient for a business's future success is the level of its workforce's commitment. How will businesses get that commitment? Having gotten it, how will they keep it?

That is the challenge Ira Jackson grapples with daily—for his employer, for himself. He has shaped the question for BankBoston and articulated it as a theme: "Managing for Value with Values."

"What companies need," Ira says, "is for people to express their personal values in the workplace. People who feel good about themselves on the job improve a company in ways the company knows instinctively that it needs to be improved. Expressing your values in the workplace is an investment in the long-term future of your company.

"Don't park your values to one side. The beauty of our economy is its diversity. There is so much talent, so many needs, so many opportunities, so many connections that need to be made between talents and needs and opportunities.

"Making the connections has magical effects. We are all capable of bringing that kind of magic to the world of business."

Work can provide the opportunity for spiritual and personal, as well as financial, growth. If it doesn't, we are wasting far too much of our lives on it.
—JAMES AUTRY

✳

Lifelines

No matter what your profession, your job, or your industry, it is up to you to bring your values to work. Integrity and corporate citizenship do not rest in the hands of a few companies or certain industries or professions. They rest in yours.

A 1998 national study concluded that the most important leadership quality is "enthusiasm." As movie mogul Samuel Goldwyn once remarked, "No person who is enthusiastic about her work has anything to fear from life."

Ask yourself: Am I bringing my whole self to work? If not, why? Is it something you can change? If not, how can you be enthusiastic?

Build your career based on values. Personal values are part

of what makes you valuable, unique in the marketplace. Don't be afraid to tell senior management what your values are, what you stand for. If they don't fit, you're probably in the wrong place. And you will never reach your potential if your values don't fit with those of your employer.

Bringing your personal values to work also means they need to be put to work for your employer. If there are things you are interested in, first do them on your own time, then build a constituency in the firm that supports them, and, finally, demonstrate why they make good business sense.

Ira Jackson could have put his values in cold storage and gone to work for whatever private company wanted to buy his talents for the biggest bucks. But he didn't.

First he built a record for public service triumphs. Then he joined a business that appreciated the commitment to the community integral to his career.

By learning to align his social programs with the bank's best interests, Ira was able to improve the bank's reputation and preserve his integrity with his own personal brand of capitalism.

**Far and away the best prize that life offers
is the chance to work hard at work worth doing.**
—Theodore Roosevelt

CHAPTER 6

✳

BUILD A DOMAIN OF LOVE

Judy George's Homecoming

───────────

A man travels the world over in search of what he needs, and returns home to find it.

—GEORGE MOORE

> In the beginning of life, when we are infants,
> we need others to survive, right? And at the end of life,
> you need others to survive, right? But here's the secret:
> In between, we need others as well.
>
> —MITCH ALBOM

In the early 1980s medical researchers at the University of Miami conducted studies on babies who were eight weeks premature. What they found out was that babies who were stroked while being fed gained weight 49 percent faster than those who were not stroked.

This "kinetic tactile stimulation," as the researchers called it—I call it simply "love"—saved hospitals $3,000 per baby before discharge. The nontechnical conclusion: Love helps us grow.

Abraham Lincoln made much the same observation, but from the viewpoint of the giver of love, when he said that "to ease another's heartache is to forget one's own." I heard that lesson best expressed by a fourteen-year-old girl named Kristen Sibilia.

Kristen was among a group of teenagers in New Paltz, New York, who were leading a discussion with parents about personal and social responsibility. I listened as Kristen discussed "altruism," which she defined as putting the needs of other family members first.

When the youngest of her two sisters questioned that notion, Kristen redefined altruism as self-interest. "Putting your needs ahead of mine is good for everybody," she said—"good for all five of us." But her little sister still didn't get it.

"If I do that," she asked, "what will I get out of it?"

"What you get out of it," Kristen explained, "is that instead of one person putting your needs first, you will have four people putting your needs first."

Life is a journey which starts at home.
—CHARLES HANDY

I start my seminars by asking a company's senior executives to spend fifteen minutes drawing pictures of the houses they grew up in. Many hesitate. They say that, as children, they moved too often to be sure which house was home.

But I keep coaxing. I'm asking them to feel home. Eventually they relax and draw.

After the scheduled fifteen minutes, which always stretches to thirty, I frequently notice a teary eye, and some people depart for the rest rooms. Old memories fill the air. All are moved.

Little decisions can be made with the head, I explain, but big decisions should be made with the heart. Now we can talk about the big things in their lives and work. The masks are off.

The most beautiful things in the world cannot be seen with the eyes, but only with the human heart.
—HELEN KELLER

I don't have to ask Judy George to draw her childhood house. A remarkable businesswoman who truly understands what's important in life, she is so real, so heartfelt, that she connects your heart to hers automatically. It's her natural instinct to do so.

Judy retreats only if she feels threatened. After all, she's still swimming with sharks in a traditional sea of male competitors.

Judy is the quintessence of class, of romance, of elegance in business. But don't misread her. She is a tigress: motivated, persistent, resilient. It is hard to imagine any other entrepreneur loving her business as much as Judy George loves hers.

Yet no matter how busy she is, how focused she must be, Judy always finds time to help others—to lend an ear, an idea, a shoulder. After all, she is the mother of four, the grandmother of five.

Judy's résumé puts her in elite company. She appears in books extolling the likes of Sam Walton and Henry Ford, both people who started their major businesses after the age of forty. She is one of only a few women who have raised a substantial amount of venture capital by themselves—and she did it without benefit of personal or family funds, a college background, or an established management team. She has run her own company for more than a decade.

But the résumé tells you little of who Judy George really is or why she is who she is. To do that, let's begin with three situations and Judy's response to "What do you do when . . ."

1. . . . you want a job badly?
2. . . . you expect the boss to promote you, but instead he fires you?
3. . . . you have a big business problem that drives you crazy day and night?

Answers:

1. Withdraw $10,000 from your husband's bank account and hire a plane to circle the chief executive's office building for one week. The plane hauls a huge banner proclaiming: "Hire Judy George. She will make you a lot of money." (It worked.)

2. Cry all night in bed. Get up in the morning. Knock on doors. Raise $30 million. Start your own business.
3. Answer will be given at the end of the chapter. Hint: It involves a family function, and guess what CEO does the arranging, cooking, and cleaning?

Judy's story is about the critical role that home plays not only in our personal lives, but in our business lives as well. Many of us talk about the importance of family, friends, and home, but the truth is, our actions reveal that work is more important. And we seldom learn what we're missing until it is too late to enjoy it.

> **I don't want to die and see on my tombstone:**
> **"He never owned a network."**
> —TED TURNER

A friend took his telephone company public in 1997. His take was tens of millions of dollars. Within a year the share price doubled.

The business grew out of his connection to a transcendental meditation community that he has belonged to for more than two decades. The community's members "honor the whole person." My friend is no longer whole, if he ever was.

He routinely misses his son's soccer games because he has to attend yet another analysts' meeting. He vowed to change by 1999. But that's what he said in 1997, too, just before going public.

Addendum: In April 1998 his entire management team walked out. Apparently my friend's benevolence in granting equity ownership to all his co-founders (the members of his TM community) led to their leaving as soon as they could legally sell their stock. The group sentiment, I'm told, was that it was time to get back to having a life again.

Within a few months the stock dropped from somewhere in the 20s to 2. In February 1999 the company filed for Chapter 11. Time now for the soccer games?

Another friend, who lives nearby in a million-dollar home, says he never imagined owning such a place. He has become a highly paid consultant and an independent one at that, all without an MBA. No easy feat.

We go to a baseball game. He tells me how the previous Sunday evening, as he was packing to leave for another weekly five-day consulting trip, his son asked him, "Daddy, why do you spend more time with them [clients] than you do with me?"

My friend was deeply touched. This first-grader has special needs. He is a sweet child. My friend talks of taking a year off—which he can now afford easily, he says. He wants to spend much of it with his wife and two children, but he especially wants to help teach his son. He promises to do it by the next fall.

In the fall he buys a new BMW sports car and plunges into working and traveling more than ever.

The man who really wants to do something finds a way; the other man finds an excuse.
—E. C. McKenzie

Yet another neighborhood friend, the mother of four, says that her father came to all her swimming meets. He never missed a single one. He couldn't stay long afterward, but her dad was always there for her. The dad? Lee Iacocca of Ford Motor Company and Chrysler Corporation fame.

"Kathy's meets went into my appointment book and were immovable," Iacocca recalls. "If you can't schedule to see your family, you probably can't manage your business well, either."

Progress? Yes. Judy George, however, would say that you don't get "strength from fitting your family into your schedule. You don't get it from other people doing the family work so you can just show up." You certainly don't start a personal relationship that way.

In graduate school my girlfriend's roommate was engaged to a much older, well-known business mogul. A personable, bright, handsome man, he traveled from New York to Cambridge, Massachusetts, to see her. She was penned—along with his accountant and Boston lawyers—into his schedule by assistants.

This young woman could see the writing on the wall: once married, he wouldn't even come to all her "swimming meets." She broke off the engagement.

The future is made of the same stuff as the present.
—SIMONE WEIL

Many people talk about taking time off to be with their families. But when? "Later," of course.

I myself used to assume that my career came first, and once I had it nailed down, quality family time would take precedence. Nonsense.

As Richard Imershein, a dear friend and highly respected retired executive at International Business Machines Corporation, told graduate students at Yale University: "Never will it be easier for you to be involved with your family or your community than early in your career. As you move up, it gets more difficult, not less. You have more corporate responsibilities. So either you have to leave the job, or establish your work and lifestyles early in your career."

In the early 1990s Dow Jones & Company's surveys of top

college graduates showed that a majority asked corporate recruiters how much time would be available for home and
hobbies. The recruiters viewed these people as "lazy."

But five years later studies revealed these home-oriented
sluggards to be the most productive professionals of their
generation. Passionate about their lives away from work,
they were also well organized, had a clear sense of priorities,
and worked at jobs they loved.

> **Home is the place where, when you have to go there,**
> **they have to take you in.**
> —ROBERT FROST

Judy George's life demonstrates that home is a source of
strength for work, not a cause of weakness. Whatever
"home" means—children, a partner, parents, or the friendly
neighborhood tavern (television's Cheers, "where everybody
knows your name")—it provides unconditional support. It
accepts you and loves you.

Judy gets her energy from home. It accepts her whether
things go well or lousy. Day after day it motivates her to meet
the challenges of being simultaneously a chief executive, a
mother, a wife, and a humanitarian.

> **All rising to a great place is by a winding stair.**
> —FRANCIS BACON

It was a beautiful morning in Milton, Massachusetts, that Sunday in 1985 when the chairman and owner of Scandinavian
Design called his company president to set up an urgent
meeting for later in the day.

The president, Judy George, had no doubt about the reason for the meeting. At long last she was going to get what she had asked for: a promotion, a raise, a piece of the company. Heaven knew she deserved it.

Arguably, Judy George was responsible for the phenomenal decade-long success of Scandinavian Design. She had built the specialty furniture chain into a $100 million business that enjoyed 15 percent pretax profit year after year. For this she had received public accolades and wide-ranging press attention that resonated throughout the industry and the world at large.

Judy was a hot property in the mid-1980s. As a professor of retailing, I would ask around, "Who are the top retail women in town?" Judy George's name was always one of the first mentioned. Now, in just a few hours, she would reap the material rewards of her success—or so she thought.

In anticipation, Judy did what she always does at key moments of her life. She called her children, her friends, her family, and invited them over for a party. When she came home from the meeting in triumph that evening, she wanted them there to help celebrate.

And she cooked. She cooked for most of the day. She prepared the house. She got everything ready, and late in the afternoon she got herself ready. Elegantly dressed, as always, she left home to meet with the owner/chairman of Scandinavian Design and claim her prize.

> **Experience is something you don't get**
> **until just after you need it.**
> **—ANONYMOUS**

He fired her. Summarily. On the spot.

Judy recounts that he "met me at the door, handed me my belongings, and said, 'You're fired.' I wasn't even allowed to come back to say good-bye to the six hundred people who worked for us, almost all of whom I had hired. It was simply: 'Take your things and go home.'"

When she arrived home, she announced to her family and friends that she didn't feel well. But she urged them to stay and eat and enjoy themselves. Then she went upstairs and lay down on her bed and wept.

"It was like a death," Judy says, vividly recalling the moment years later. "I had been so focused on making the company great, and now I had been ripped away from it. I knew all the people there intimately, and they were all still part of the company, and I was out. It was devastating."

All night long Judy mourned her loss, her sense of rejection, the seeming repudiation of her strengths and achievements. The suddenness of the blow was like the knockout punch the fighter never sees coming—as boxing's former heavyweight champion Mike Tyson once said when told that an opponent had a plan to beat him: "They all got a plan— until they get hit."

Judy had been hit. But she's never down for the count. Not Judy George. And she had a plan for after the punch, too.

"The next morning," she says with great pride, "I got up and started my whole new life and career."

> **People say I don't take criticism well, but I say,**
> **"What the hell do they know?"**
> —GROUCHO MARX

Judy reflects today on the experience: "I was so focused on me, on being successful, that I didn't see what was going on around me. I was as much at fault for many things as I was a reason for the company's success.

"As Henry Ford once said, 'Failure is the opportunity to begin again more intelligently.' He's right. It was time for me to go home—time to feel the pain and move on to what I wanted to do in the first place: have my own home furnishings company."

Judy went out and raised capital for her own creation, Domain, Inc. The business grew organically out of who and what Judy is. What's more, Domain offered its customers a chance to be who and what they are and allowed co-workers to do the same.

Judy dedicated the same explosive energy to Domain that she has put into every venture she has launched since opening her first lemonade stand at the age of five. As always, she resolutely built and crossed all sorts of bridges. But her efforts would not have succeeded without the sustaining love of friends, new and old, without the nourishing energy of family and home.

> **There are two lasting bequests we can hope to give our children. One is roots; the other, wings.**
> —HODDING CARTER

The daughter of an Italian mother and Lebanese father in Quincy, Massachusetts, Judy felt like an outsider in her neighborhood. She also believed she got less attention than her siblings.

Often left behind while her parents tried to start their own chrome-polishing business, Judy felt abandoned—even though she was sent to stay with a dancer and a sculptor who lived a Bohemian life, entertaining all types of creative people.

"I think at that very young age, I started building the bridges toward never being left by anybody again," Judy says.

She grew up wanting to save everybody else. "I was always Tarzan saving Jane." At sixteen, wanting to save people from polio, Judy became the young adult chairman of the March of Dimes. "There was this passion," she says. "When I got an idea or a vision, I had to go out and do it."

She raised more than $10,000 for the March of Dimes but was nearly arrested because she didn't have the proper paperwork: How could a kid raise that sort of money, anyway? And what was that money really for?

Judy's unusual success attracted media attention. So instead of being arrested, she became a celebrity. She was thrilled. Her parents concluded that they had a wild one on their hands.

After Judy graduated high school, her parents arranged a marriage to Simon George. "My parents picked a man I never would have married," Judy acknowledges. "But my mother knew me. Today, nearly forty years later, I realize how smart she was."

Simon was a calming influence, as were the four children born over the next six years. Judy had no time for anything but home and hearth. Still, she never stopped dreaming and creating.

> **You see things, and you say, "Why?" But I dream things**
> **that never were, and I say, "Why not?"**
> —GEORGE BERNARD SHAW

Once her youngest was in school, Judy was ready to go, but where? "No one would hire a mother of four with no education. I wanted to continue my passion for home design, so I started my own consulting company, Ideas By George."

She parlayed that venture into a newspaper column. Then, after submitting a complete script and marketing layout, she got her own local television show, *Designer in the House.*

Judy kept looking for more, "filled with strength," as she puts it, from her family. But there remained many barriers for women in the industry, particularly for women with children.

Yearning to run the design studio for a major company, she got an interview. But the president simply laughed at her and said: "You don't have the right degrees. You've never even been in the business. Why would I want to hire you for this job?"

Judy went home, got Simon's bankbook, and took $10,000 out of his account. She hired a plane to fly around the president's office for a week, towing a banner that blazed a Judy George–style message: "Hire Judy George. She will make you a lot of money."

He hired her. She made him a lot of money.

> **If you think you can, you can.**
> **If you think you can't, you're right.**
> —MARY KAY ASH

Judy's two big breaks were still ahead of her. The first came in 1975 when she was hired by Hamilton, Inc., to run its design department. When Hamilton was acquired in 1976 by Scandinavian Design, she got the same job at that healthier, larger company. She learned, got industry experience, and became the company's well-known and respected president.

The second came when she was fired by Scandinavian Design in 1985, which allowed her to launch Domain with the opening of two Boston stores in the fall of 1986.

Failure and success are perhaps the two hardest things to handle in life. But as Dee Hock, the architect of Visa International, once said, the real failure is "not to fall short of all you might dream, but to fall short of dreaming all you might realize."

And Scandinavian Design had encouraged Judy to dream.

It established her in the industry—the only woman president—and the support of the owner enabled her to achieve important breakthroughs.

Judy George may have wept the night away that Sunday, but after ten years at Scandinavian Design, all was in place: her passion for enterprise, the personal relationships to sustain that passion, and the experience, know-how, contacts, and reputation within the industry.

If the love of family and friends got her out of bed the morning after she was fired, it was what Simon calls his wife's "plain, simple courage" that got her in front of venture capitalists.

> **You can't be brave if you've only had**
> **wonderful things happen to you.**
> —MARY TYLER MOORE

Passion like Judy's that burns white hot cannot sustain itself forever without some sort of refueling. The personal connection always refueled Judy. Whatever business she was in, it was really a people business, "the business of being human," as she puts it. "Success isn't about an idea or concept. It's about people."

Now was the time to start the business she had always wanted and to run it her way: "No rules, nothing in front of me, no how-tos—so I could explore the very best of who I was." The guiding business principles of this new venture would be "what I can live with and what excites me." It would be her own domain.

And what was Judy George's domain if not the home? What was her business if not finding new ways to make a home beautiful and make it better?

Home was always where Judy belonged. Home was always her vision of enterprise. Home was where her family and friends kindled the very stuff and materials that kept Judy George's passion burning brightly. It was a passion from deep inside.

Judy was ready to fly: "The business I wanted to be in is all about home and self-improvement and self-expression. I wanted to improve the quality of how people live. I wanted to build something that helped people feel really good about themselves."

She set out to "design a concept that could touch each individual, could help them understand who they are and, at the same time, fix their home so that their marriage is better, their kids are happier, and so on."

To help articulate that concept for her business plan, Judy took a tape recorder and waited outside furniture stores and department stores to interview shoppers. "What did you buy?" she asked. "Are you pleased? What was your shopping experience like?"

Without exception, people were dissatisfied. They were dissatisfied with the style of salesmanship (which they invariably found sleazy); with the shopping environment (dirty stores and unappealing displays); with the products (poor quality and design); with the prices (high).

Armed with the tapes, Judy presented herself to venture capitalists. She convinced them. She even got a big accounting firm to do the financial projections for the business plan pro bono. She did it, she believes, mostly by connecting with their feelings.

Whoever heard of thinking about the feelings of venture capitalists?

"I did research so I knew who these venture capitalists were and what they wanted to do. I only went to those who could connect with what I could bring to the table—a new concept that was right for the moment, right for the women's market that the industry needed to attract to keep growing."

Domain, Inc., was born.

**In order to create, there must be a dynamic force,
and what force is more dynamic than love?**
—IGOR STRAVINSKY

It was a concept of fashionable home furnishings—akin to a designer clothing approach at affordable prices—that could grow. One that could, and would, be widely imitated. That's because the choices in Domain let everybody be who they are.

Domain has grown into a $60 million company with twenty-three stores in seven states and plans for sixty-five more. Judy has become a brand franchise: author, motivational speaker, board director. Judy's *The Domain Book of Intuitive Home Design* led the press to call her "the Freud of home design."

Still, the road has had its bumps along the way. Growth has lagged behind what the venture capitalists hoped for thirteen years ago. They have not backed away, however, nor has Judy jumped ship—despite numerous invitations to move on.

"When the going gets tough," she says, "I get going." She digs in with that same passionate tenacity that got her up and moving the day after the worst day of her life.

"There's something to be said for taking the pain, exploring it, and getting through to the other side of it," she explains. And there's something to be said for loyalty to the people who work with her at Domain and her investors. "They have been there for me. I am there for them," Judy says simply.

For Judy George, the personal side is everything. She has remained free of the disease of "more" that complicates life and relationships. She is content to make less money and be less rich, less powerful, less everything.

As she says, "Less still gives me a chance to do things I've only dreamed about. In the end, the real issue is to live a rich life. I live a very rich life."

The family is the country of the heart.
—Giuseppe Mazzini

Judy's story concludes with a breakfast I had with her on February 12, 1998. That's where I learned the answer to question number three posed at the start of this chapter. I began to understand the depth of Judy's commitment to her life philosophy.

She had been through some very tough business months. Unexpectedly, the previous week, her president had resigned and a significant unfavorable error in the 1997 financial results was found. In addition, she had to fire her head of merchandising—a close friend, well liked, and valued as a team member for over a decade. Worse yet, many Domain executives were in revolt over his dismissal.

Such a week would have knocked most people down for the count. But not Judy. Though she looked harried and sleepless, I marveled at her resiliency as I listened to her proactive, positive alternatives that morning.

Then I asked her what she was doing for Valentine's Day. She said she was leaving work early that day to begin preparations for a party she was giving. I sat back, stunned.

In the midst of it all, Judy was leaving early on Thursday and staying home all day Friday to cook up a feast for a Valentine's Day party for her thirty-year-old daughter, Jennifer, on Saturday.

Who arranged the party, sent out the invitations, and confirmed fifty people? One of Judy's assistants? No, CEO Judy George did. Don't most chief executives do this? Particularly in tough business times?

Judy George cooks for her four grown-up children and

helps arrange birthday parties for her grandchildren. This is where Judy George comes from. It's who she is. This is the source of her resiliency, the fountain of her strength.

Judy insists: "You never will find time for anything. You must make the time for what's important to you. And, I know, you get strength from being family in all the little things, moment by moment."

> **To keep the lamp burning,**
> **we have to keep putting oil in it.**
> —MOTHER TERESA

I think about that breakfast a lot. I think about what I say I do with my time and what I really do with it. I question my either/or assumptions about energy. I consider how I return from each retreat, each vacation, and fall into the same patterns.

When friends talk of how the workplace treats them as dispensable and how they think of themselves and how they want to be indispensable, I think, Are we forgetting where we are truly indispensable? Where long-distance strength really comes from?

In building Domain, Inc., Judy George has built her business as her home and her home as her business. It's her own domain of acceptance and much love.

> **To be happy at home**
> **is the ultimate result of all ambition.**
> —SAMUEL JOHNSON

✳

Lifelines

Thomas Merton believed that "if you have love, you will do all things well." Ask yourself, how often do you give out love to your family and friends and let love in?

Supportive relationships sustain us through life. They accept the good with the bad. As Oprah Winfrey remarked, "Lots of people want to ride with you in the limo, but what you want is someone who will take the bus with you when the limo breaks down."

Judy George is a model of resiliency. She is also a model of how important a strong relationship with one's family is to success in the workplace. Time with the family is not time away from work, not time to be scheduled in an appointment book. It is time that helps strengthen one's effectiveness as a leader, manager, entrepreneur . . . and human being.

The more supportive relationships you can develop, the more energy you will have to persevere and achieve in your career—and the more opportunity you will have to live a life of significance. To whom are we more significant, more irreplaceable, than our family?

Family is a way of holding hands with forever.
—Noah ben Shea

PART 3

✴

WHAT CAN YOU DO?

Develop Market Value

CHAPTER 7

✳

CREATE YOUR PLATFORM AND LEAP

David Berge's Handiwork

**We are what we repeatedly do.
Excellence, then, is not an act, but a habit.**
—ARISTOTLE

> Only those who will risk going too far
> can possibly find out how far one can go.
> —T. S. ELIOT

On the South Pacific island of Pentecost, men still practice land diving, an ancient ritual to please the gods and ensure a good yam harvest. Each builds his own diving platform against a tree, preferably on a slope, with plenty of flat space below for landing.

The diver chooses the site carefully, cuts and shapes the sapling trunks, braces the tower with branches, and lashes the whole thing together with liana vines. He and he alone is responsible for the construction. No other person can be held responsible for any mishaps, and no one else can receive credit for the diver's success.

The diver also selects his own diving vines, looking for exactly the right length to brake his headfirst plunge just as his hair brushes the ground. Too long a vine can mean a fatal crash landing; too short a vine will bounce the diver back up to his platform, yo-yo style, with possibly harmful consequences for the harvest.

On the appointed day, the diver climbs the tower, which may be anywhere from sixty-five to eighty-five feet high, ties on the vine he has chosen, steps onto his platform—at the tapered tower's narrowest point—and leaps. That is, unless he has second thoughts or gets cold feet.

In the island's Melanesian culture, no shame attaches to a diver who changes his mind at the last moment, for whatever reason. Other divers will take his place to ensure the year's harvest. The reluctant diver can try again next year; his tower will still be there.

To be successful, have your heart in your business, and your business in your heart.
—THOMAS WATSON

For more than a decade I have urged students and executives to build a career platform based on their passions and then trust in its strength. I believe that if you develop skills you truly enjoy exercising, you can take off to just about anywhere.

This means divorcing your career thinking from the typical corporate, quarterly time horizon. Rather, construct your career more like the diving towers of Pentecost—supported by the tree of your life, from the ground up, with passion and painstaking attention to detail.

Can you make that platform unique, of value in the marketplace? Yes, if it truly reflects you and is something you are willing to work on.

I often illustrate my ideas with the story of an engineer who developed an exceptional gift for fixing complex machines. He loved his work and spent many happy years at one company. Eventually he left to pursue his own interests.

Less than a year later he got a call from his former employer. It seemed that no one could fix a multimillion-dollar machine. Could he please try? Reluctantly the engineer put aside his own work to take up the challenge.

He spent a day studying the huge machine. At the end of the workday he marked an "x" in chalk on a particular component and declared with certainty, "This is where your problem is." The part was replaced, and sure enough, the machine worked perfectly.

When the company received the engineer's bill for

$50,000, it demanded an itemized accounting of his charges. His brief response read as follows:

One chalk mark $1.00
Knowing where to put it $49,999.00

The bill was paid in full.

For every complex problem, there is a simple solution that is elegant, easy to understand, and wrong.
—H. L. MENCKEN

Although my students invariably enjoy the story of the engineer, they nevertheless have come up with three qualifications over the years: One, there are many ways to build a platform; two, as marketplace conditions change, the value of that platform will vary; and three, just because you have a platform doesn't mean you will leap.

As is always the case, the students teach the teacher.

I built my own platform by being good at school. (Nearly twenty years at Harvard opens many doors.) I became adept at computers and marketing, but in the early 1990s I, too, had to retool.

As one of my close friends, a high-ranking Fortune 50 refugee, puts it: "Many of us followed the money, developed what the marketplace and specific companies wanted, and found that our passion wasn't there. The pain got great enough, and the dissatisfaction deep enough with a life devoid of meaning, that we finally broke out.

"Today, education is our security, the promise of our right livelihood. It allows us to get better at what we love. We no longer put off constructing our platform, and we don't rely on others to do it for us. We are much less likely to compromise on what is truly important to us. I just wish I hadn't waited so long."

> **What each must seek in his life ... is something out of his own unique potentiality for experience, something that never has been and never could have been experienced by anyone else.**
> —JOSEPH CAMPBELL

David Berge is my teacher of platform building and leap taking. He started instinctively building his tower of creativity as a youngster, growing up in the Spam capital of the world, Austin, Minnesota, home to the Hormel Foods Corporation and a division of the Weyerhaeuser Company.

David likes to camp and take sabbaticals for months at a time—alone with books, his thoughts, and the great outdoors. A lover of the art of storytelling and of fiction—"fiction weaves history, experience, reality, and dreams to tell some greater truth," he declares—David is a disciple of Emersonian self-reliance and of Henry David Thoreau's rustic, natural simplicity.

When I first met David in 1991, I saw him as one of those unassuming men who look and feel uncomfortable in suits and ties. When you learn that he's a banking executive, you wonder who is kidding whom. But as he points out, using an old expression, "You can't judge a book by its cover."

If you ask him about his work, you might be treated to a response something like this: "Is it riskier to lend money a) to a higher-income family for its third boat or second home; or b) to a lower-income family for their first home? Answer: a). That first home is the only place the lower-income family has to live, and their commitment to pay that loan is going to be very high."

That's what David does. It's also who he is.

All progress depends on the unreasonable man.
The reasonable man adapts himself to the world.
The unreasonable man persists in trying
to adapt the world to himself.
—GEORGE BERNARD SHAW

David is in the business of changing people's perceptions—that is, changing traditional bankers' perceptions about money and community lending; about small business, affordable housing projects, organic farms, schools, environmental projects; about small and complicated loans.

With no special pedigree from famous institutions of education or commerce, David built his platform by selling vacuum cleaners door to door and working in small nonprofit organizations before falling into the world of commercial banking. Then, as director of the Vermont National Bank's Socially Responsible Banking (SRB) Fund, he turned the banking industry's assumptions about community lending upside down.

The SRB Fund allows depositors to earmark their money for loans to small local enterprises that are deemed to have a positive impact on the community. As its steward, David has based his career on risk—his own and others'. It didn't faze him.

A few years ago Vermont National Bank was honored with a highly prestigious award from the Business Enterprise Trust. The award ceremonies are attended by the likes of President Bill Clinton and hosted by celebrities such as Barbara Walters.

When the bank's SRB Fund was recognized at the 1996 ceremony, Bill Moyers commented: "A state of small towns, Yankee traditions, and down-home values, Vermont seems an unlikely place for a revolution in banking. Yet in 1989 one of the most daring innovations in commercial lending was launched here, in Brattleboro."

To know David you must know this: When the award was first offered, it was designated for David Berge at the Vermont National Bank. But David refused to be singled out. He requested that the award go solely to the bank.

David's story is one of a practical philosopher who cares less about interpreting the world and more about changing it, one family at a time.

> **Whatever you can do or dream you can, begin it.**
> **Boldness has genius, power, and magic in it.**
> —JOHANN WOLFGANG VON GOETHE

I have wondered how this contrarian dealt so well with the risks inherent in aggressive lending to unconventional borrowers for the express purpose of advancing social goals. It was David Berge's reputation alone that guaranteed these low-margin loans to projects that other bankers would either reject out of hand or consider doing at maybe 15 percent to 18 percent, not the 8 percent or 9 percent the SRB Fund charges.

David was only thirty years old when he arrived at Vermont National Bank in 1990 and decided to reinvent the lending process—and himself along with it. How could he be so sure of himself? So sure of his abilities to shape a job and a life out of his passion for helping to finance small community businesses dedicated to making a social and financial impact?

Banks care about *money*, right? So here's how bankers explained David's success in the award citation: "David's secret combines hard financial analysis with lots of flexibility and a determination to help socially responsible businesses through collaborating with borrowers to make the loans work and using intermediaries to increase loan volume."

Technically that analysis was correct. And by doing that,

David created a new model of community lending that boosted the bank's deposits and loans, differentiated the bank in the marketplace, brought the bank national attention, and strengthened the Green Mountain State's communities.

But David puts it differently. He defines his success in the more personal terms of the individual, the passion, the purpose.

"If I could create a job for you, what would you do?" queries David the philosopher. "What I like to hear is, 'My work is meaningful to me, and this is what I am interested in,' not, 'I'd give anything to do what you're doing.' Too many people put off the hard decision—to do what they want to do.

"It's a myth to think skills create work," he goes on. "It is the work that creates the skills. Don't think about where you work, but about the direction the work is leading you. Ask yourself: Are you learning from the work itself? Is it creating value—to you, to the company, to the community? Think of your workplace as a support community for learning."

Often people attempt to live their life backwards. They try to have more things or more money to do more of what they want, so they will be happier. The way it actually works is in reverse. You must first be who you really are, then do what you need to do to have what you want.
—MARGARET YOUNG

This slightly built, unconventional banker drills on intensely with a series of questions.

David asks in a steely, staccato manner: How many compromises have you made before you even get to the workplace? How many options did you eliminate on your way to your current job, thinking only about a 10 percent change (like more flextime) instead of a limitless range of possibilities?

How far are you already from your passion? How many bargains did you strike with yourself? How many rationalizations have you made for postponing what you really want to do, like "I'll make the money for x number of years, and then . . ."?

David says his industry changed more in the past five to ten years than in the last hundred years put together. And when value changes, how you think of your value in the marketplace must change, too.

"There is no one way to keep up," he says. "Only your way, built on a platform of what you care about, what you hunger for, what you are willing to fight for. The trick then is to think of yourself not as an asset—after all, assets depreciate—but as an income generator."

How do you become an income generator? How do you really differentiate yourself in the marketplace? A business friend of David's and mine provides perspective.

"Our talents and skills are similar," he says. "It is the combination of them, the music and the magic of who we are—as it is played with others, heard by others—that makes us, and our offerings, unique."

To offer something different, be something different. To be something different, be what you want to be. Just keep testing, adding. As Ralph Waldo Emerson observed: "All life is an experiment. The more experiments you make, the better."

David sums up: "All you really have are three things—your creativity, energy, and integrity. Continue to nourish those three things, and you'll continue to be a valuable contributor whatever the workplace, whatever the particular job requirements."

What was silent in the father speaks in the son.
—FRIEDRICH WILHELM NIETZSCHE

If you were one of the thirty thousand residents of Austin, Minnesota, when David was growing up, you or someone in your family probably worked at a local company like Hormel or Weyerhaeuser. And you were either pro-company or pro-union.

The Berge family supported David and his four sisters by working at both companies. David's dad was a union worker at Weyerhaeuser. His mother worked at Hormel, where office workers like herself were not included in the union. She had a good reputation as a cost analyst and kept her mind on doing her work well. When the union called a strike, office workers were told to go to work. If you were late, your pay was docked.

Dad's dream was to be a history teacher and a coach. It just didn't happen. Instead he became known for his excellent work as a machinist at Weyerhaeuser and was the plant's highest-paid worker. He was also very active in the union.

When his father hurt his shoulder at work, he stayed on, but the company didn't treat him well. He was rewarded with daily latrine duty. Even then he continued to pursue his one goal—do the highest-quality work.

David spent much of his childhood with friends or wrapped up in a book. Austin was a good town to grow up in. After he was grown and gone, however, Austin in the 1980s became the site of bitter Hormel strikes that polarized what was otherwise a close-knit community.

> **Knowing others is wisdom;**
> **knowing yourself is enlightenment.**
> —LAO-TZU

David went to St. John's University in Collegeville, Minnesota. He ran track and cross-country, enjoying the woods and the lakes. He didn't declare a major but looked for the best professors and studied what they taught, which included government, humanities, and German. One month before graduation he finally declared a triple major, having qualified in all three of his areas of study.

David always recognized and zealously attended to his own need for "quiet time"—time off, time away, time spent somewhere else.

"It seems we keep filling our brain and never empty it," he muses. "We keep draining our energy, without filling it. I need to stop from time to time and check in on three things: my creativity, energy, and integrity. They require upkeep."

For his first job right out of college, David sought something that would earn him enough money in a short enough time to allow him to take the winter off. He had lots of books waiting to be read.

The job he got was selling vacuum cleaners, using a pitch scripted down to the last comma and from which no deviations were allowed. Despite days that began with everyone standing on chairs, singing company songs—"How much is that Kirby in the window?"—David found the comedy and sometimes the humility in the job a means to an end. Still, his three months of trying to sweet-talk his way into people's homes to sell them vacuums taught him a great deal about how unsung millions feel and hope, live and die.

"Everyone should sell door to door," David says. "You learn what people really talk about, what really happens, the rough edges.

"It was a sobering experience," he goes on. "You wouldn't believe how many people are lonely, watching soap operas all afternoon or drinking by themselves at noon. We spent time together. We talked about decency, about parenthood, about community.

"I was careful not to sell a system to a family that I could see couldn't afford it. Some would want to buy one just to thank me for being nice to them."

You have to stay in shape. My grandmother started walking five miles a day when she was sixty. She's ninety-seven today, and we don't know where the hell she is.
—ELLEN DEGENERES

David took his newly won knowledge, a suitcase full of books, and three months' worth of sales commissions to a small cabin in northern Minnesota. That winter of reading, watching the deer running across the frozen lake, and listening to the wolves howl was his first sabbatical.

"I came out of the woods very happy," he says. "I needed to give context to my experiences, to not let the gap become too great between a head full of information and what I did with it. I could then fill some gaps in my skill set of things I care about. It was great to be reading again, building up my energy.

"I became convinced that sabbaticals had to be a permanent part of my life," David goes on. "I also decided on my next step, a move to 'the Cities.'" (That's Minnesota talk for Minneapolis/St. Paul.)

At the time, David's plan could not even be called a first draft; his passion was still embryonic. All he knew was that he was going to spend some time working for a nonprofit organization.

The trouble with most of us is that we know too much that ain't so.
—MARK TWAIN

With what he describes as "the naïveté only a young person can have," David walked into the Minneapolis City Hall and knocked on the first door he found. "I'd like to go to work for a nonprofit organization," he declared to the startled city employee who greeted him. "What can you recommend?"

The civil servant thought for a moment, then referred David to another office down the hall. There he was referred to a third office, where someone sent him to knock on yet another door, behind which was a man who recommended a small neighborhood organization in north Minneapolis.

So began his career. This may be why David Berge is convinced that "doors will always be open for you, but at a price."

"We underestimate people's willingness to help," David says. "Giving is a wonderful gift. I'll bet more people fail by never asking than by being refused help. So if the door feels right, walk on through. How else can you find your own way? How else to create your own platform?"

David's career advice continues: "If you don't want companies to think quarterly, why should you think that way in your career choices? There are a lot of people who, if they ran their companies the way they run their careers, would run them into the ground.

"Your career is not a quarterly event with a ninety-day goal," he cautions. "It's a lifetime of making a living while you make a life. Think of it that way, and that's the way you'll live it out."

To climb steep hills requires a slow pace at first.
—WILLIAM SHAKESPEARE

That first door David walked through took him to a small community organization that was developing a leadership effectiveness training program. He signed on and was soon learning to identify the skills, tools, and models that worked to effect change as well as those that did not.

He had not yet defined his life's passion, but he thought

that "this context of doing the right thing from a place of personal integrity" was at least consistent with his values and personal needs.

Other doors opened. While pursuing graduate studies at the Humphrey Institute of Public Affairs, David went to talk with Willis Bright at the Honeywell Corporation in its corporate community responsibility department. He still remembers Willis asking, "If I created a job today for you here to do anything, what would you do?"

By the end of the meeting he had a job helping piece together a skills-based training program for minorities, women, and veterans.

Next David researched the feasibility of creating secondary markets for small-business loans in Minnesota, finding out what kinds of loan pools were available, who was lending to small businesses, what worked, what didn't. After filing that report, David was hired by the University of Minnesota to work on a project analyzing small-business incubators to find out the most effective ways these businesses could create jobs.

Slowly but surely, David Berge was beginning to find his way toward structuring loans for community organizations. He discovered that money—specifically the lack of access to capital—is perceived as being central to an organization's ability to survive and to achieve its goals. Money was typically the culprit.

Still, as David explains, "No money problems are truly just money problems. But people always identify money as the issue. Dealing with money allows me to get at the true problems—the real organizational risks versus the perceived risks."

Change and growth take place when a person has risked himself and dares to become involved with his own life.
—HERBERT OTTO

After David finished graduate school, a friend suggested he talk to "an interesting guy" in Massachusetts who headed up the Institute for Community Economics (ICE). ICE was assembling a national association of community development loan funds.

By the time David responded, the staff positions had already been filled. Even so, the institute's leader agreed to interview David, and in a burst of spontaneity, he asked, "How would you like to be our senior loan officer?"

Surprised by the offer, David replied, "I've never really made a loan." He then added, "But here's what I do and here's how I think."

He got the job. From day one he enjoyed the three years he spent practicing how to make loans and help nonprofit community organizations become workable investments. "I learned that there is no one set of cures, something you can easily replicate, a single model. Models aren't the starting point; they are the result of understanding the issues and the process."

Loan officer David Berge continued to take his "time away." In fact, doing so eventually became a condition of accepting work. He worked a crazy schedule when he was there, then took off to read fiction, to "learn more about the magical art of storytelling and about being human."

"Reading nurses the part of me that thinks and creates," David says. "Fiction stands at the dividing line of describing events as they actually happened versus as symbols of underlying personal truths."

At ICE he also learned how to help nonprofits "test the reality of what they needed to know to get financing." He discovered that the indirect benefit of a loan—helping the organization itself down the line—could be as important as the direct benefit. And he learned that there is no correlation between income and capability.

"There are people who are out there doing what they do

well. They have the passion," David says. "They're going to find a way no matter what."

German philosopher Georg Wilhelm Hegel once said that "nothing good in the world has been accomplished without passion." David Berge's passion was to drive people beyond the simply possible all the way to what would work better.

"Be driven by your passion," exhorts David, "but be really focused on effectiveness. Motivation doesn't guarantee implementation."

In 1989 Vermont National Bank launched its Socially Responsible Banking Fund. A year later deposits were strong, but lending was difficult. It was time to lure David Berge to Vermont. He had built his platform. Now he was ready to make the leap into commercial banking.

> **I am looking for a lot of men who have
> an infinite capacity to not know what can't be done.**
> —HENRY FORD

"You must answer two questions to be effective in creating the change you want," begins David. "You can't just ask, 'How will I be effective?'—it's too big and vague—so first you need to break it down to a scale that you can understand, like 'How will I get my neighbor to paint his house?' Second, 'How do you sustain this?' Time after time I would run into the issue of organizations not being prepared to succeed."

David faced the immediate challenge of integrating the new fund into traditional lending practices and changing stubborn prejudices in the banking world. He had entered a world that hates the word *exception* when placed next to the word *loan*. All exceptions are bad, because once you go outside normal policy, it means risk. David had to figure out how to remove his loans from the "exceptions" category.

"I remember the senior credit officer asking me about a

zero percent loan that I had approved, and whether we were going to see many of them. I explained that a depositor had agreed to place a zero percent deposit to support that loan, and that's what the borrower could afford.

"I needed to change perceptions, make this type of lending seem natural, in order to get my banking colleagues— Vermont bankers—to change traditional behaviors."

**There is nothing more difficult to carry out,
nor more doubtful of success, nor more dangerous
to handle, than to initiate a new order of things.**
—NICCOLÒ MACHIAVELLI

Vermont is a state of mind. It has a soul—a spiritual presence—that is unique. A sense of permanence fills the air.

Vermont ways are a throwback to the days when people bartered rather than bought, when you knew your neighbors and they knew you. Connections between families go back at least a few generations. Eighteen years in Vermont still labels you a "newcomer." Trust evolves with time.

It is said that wealth isolates the wealthy, making many people invisible to the rich. With little concentration of wealth, Vermonters know one another, care about one another, feel responsible for one another. There's an unspoken acknowledgment of community and its central importance in individual lives.

Vermonters understand what Abraham Lincoln meant when he said: "The better part of one's life consists of his friendships." The social fabric is dependent on personal relationships. Transactions are often relationship based, and integrity serves as social currency.

David observes that Vermonters are part of a community in which it is as if everyone lives next door. "Vermont is so small that we don't even use people's last names in conversation," he notes with pleasure. "A typical exchange might go something like this: 'I heard from Andy, after the meeting with Gus, that Amy's worried about the rate on that project up in Burlington.'"

**We talk about the quality of product and service.
What about the quality of our relationships
and the quality of our communications
and the quality of our promises to each other?**
—MAX DE PREE

David knew instinctively that sustainability was important, not just in Vermont, but in banking in general. "As a lender, when I talk about sustainability, it means that if I want a loan to work for thirty years, I have to figure out how the life of that organization moves over a period of time, and I have to accommodate that in the loan structure.

"By the same token, the bank management, looking at the structure of the loan, sees the deposits I've brought in to support the deal and the low delinquencies; that's their sustainability," he explains.

Each loan attracts five times itself in deposits. But what is the product? Money? David understands that "money per se doesn't really have a value, it doesn't really exist. It exists as the value between things. And that value is built on understanding people and their relationships."

It didn't take long in Vermont for people to hear that David would drive all the way across the state after work, work with customers on their kitchen table all night, sleep on their couch, and drive again in the morning. He quickly became known as the "midnight banker."

What David accomplished at the bank far transcends money. In 1997 the SRB Fund totaled $172 million and had eighteen thousand depositors from forty-two states and sixteen countries. More than 75 percent of its depositors were new to Vermont National Bank. And though the fund accounted for only 9 percent of the bank's assets, its dollar growth in both loans and deposits over the eight-year period exceeded that of the rest of the bank.

"You earn the same interest, have the same access, but you know you are helping Joe down the street," comments one depositor.

**It is not because things are difficult that we do not dare.
It is because we do not dare that they are difficult.**
—LUCIUS ANNAEUS SENECA

To a venture still finding its way, David brought a creative vision for new methods of doing things—new to both banks and nonprofit organizations. Asked to reconceptualize the loan-making process for the SRB Fund, he effectively reconceptualized a model for financing socially minded organizations.

David was able to decrease the risk with flexible underwriting and loan terms, and that same flexibility dramatically improved the performances of the loans. It is a complicated process based on the use of a network of intermediaries whom David got to know over the years and in-depth knowledge of potential borrowers—knowledge he gained from neighborhood barbecues as much as anywhere else.

David realizes that "as banking has changed, loan growth and performance have become more important. We needed an approach that would re-create relationships and trust. You have to determine, for example, whether the borrower fully understands what he must do to be successful."

Today David is reinventing his job again, figuring out how he can generate more value with other financial instruments. For one thing, he wants to create an equity pool to encourage the kind of behavior he would like to see, in both the workplace and the community.

In fact, David thinks of his own workplace as "a community, a web of relationships. I look at workplaces like a lender, asking not 'How does it work when it's working well?' but 'How does it work when it's not working?'"

And David keeps learning from the community of the workplace and from giving back to the community. The same is true for the way he makes a living and the way he makes his life: he keeps growing, learning, testing limits, trying new things.

Money and community—*and*, not *or*. By reconciling supposed opposites, David is not only successful on the outside, he's pretty full on the inside, too, which means it's time for another sabbatical. After that, David will, no doubt, be ready to leap to his next challenge.

> **Ah, but a man's reach should exceed his grasp,**
> **or what's a heaven for?**
> —ROBERT BROWNING

✷

Lifelines

Are you developing your value in the marketplace and regularly testing its limits? Do you know how you are making your company more successful?

You don't need a résumé featuring brand-name educational institutions or corporate icons to build a personal platform of employability, to create your value in the marketplace, and to test that value and stretch it. You do need to trust your passion and develop it.

Know what you stand for, develop what you want to be

good at, and make sure the market values it. If you know the work that you love, the skills you need will be apparent.

Moreover, ensuring your effectiveness requires focus and dedication—step by step. It follows the natural law known to any good banker and expressed by Albert Einstein: "The most powerful force in the world? Compound interest."

David Berge's passion for small environmental and community-based businesses, and his hunger for fairness, led him to develop a complex skill for making market-rate loans available to these businesses. His innovative lending method, remarkable for its intimacy and respect for others, owed as much to his stint as a door-to-door salesman as to his early experience as a loan officer.

In fact, it was his "soft" people skills as much as his "hard" financial skills that made David Berge's leap more like a natural next step.

Be great in the little things.
—GEORGE HERBERT PALMER

CHAPTER 8

✸

SEEK COMMON GROUND FOR UNCOMMON RESULTS

Mike Barr's Vision

───────────

Only connect.

—E. M. FORSTER

**The problem with communication
is the illusion that it has occurred.**
—GEORGE BERNARD SHAW

Hiking alone in Yellowstone Park one spring day, a young Jewish man suddenly encounters a huge, menacing grizzly bear. He immediately panics and runs, shedding one article of clothing at a time, hoping to distract the bear. It doesn't work.

Instead, the bear remains focused on his prey, coming after the man at a quickening pace.

Nearly naked, the young man spots a deserted cabin, stumbles inside, and slams the door shut. Saved! He collapses in relief and exhaustion.

Still shaken, he begins praying in Hebrew, thanking God for sparing his life. His prayers are interrupted by the sounds of the bear outside the door. The bear is also praying in Hebrew.

Amazed, the young man opens the door to welcome in what is surely one of God's special creatures. The bear lumbers in, crouches down next to the man, and they continue praying together. Yes, the oddest of brethren, but who knows God's plan? What a blessing!

Pondering this miracle of miracles, the young man continues, entranced in prayer, until he hears the bear move, apparently finishing his last prayer. He listens closely to the unmistakable words—*"Hamotzee lechem mein h'aretz"*— the Jewish prayer of thanks to God for the food you are about to eat.

156

The most exciting breakthrough of the twenty-first century will occur not because of technology, but because of an expanding concept of what it means to be human.
—JOHN NAISBITT

Do you ever have the nagging feeling that any day now out there in corporate America, you, too, may become lunch for some deceptively pious bear? If so, you're not alone. Hundreds of high-pressured managers spend their careers peering over their shoulders, feeling as if they are being chased by wild animals.

Why do we endure this Pentium-paced business life? We are continually pushed to be more productive, work longer hours, be available electronically all the time, and see our families less . . . or we're out. Maybe we're out anyway. It's exhausting, and it's also frightening.

In this technocratic jungle, with its delete-or-be-deleted morality, a wonderfully sane person reinforces for me the importance of "soft" skills in creating a successful career and a happier life. He is Mike Barr, a man who owes his livelihood—indeed, his very life—to the power of persuasive communication.

Mike Barr is the child of Ukrainian Jews who escaped from a German Nazi labor camp and certain death. Fleeing through southern Russia, they survived from day to day by picking up the dialect of each town along their route. Their lives depended on their ability to identify with total strangers. So to blend in with the locals, they learned to communicate in the words and sounds of others.

Born in postwar Paris, Mike spent his childhood witnessing the tumultuous birth of the modern state of Israel. Later he lived in Cuba when Fidel Castro came to power, in the United States as John Kennedy lifted the nation's spirits, and in Canada with young Americans opposed to the Vietnam War. In Israel he served as a soldier in the Yom Kippur War,

157

and in New York he participated in the madness and greed of Wall Street in the 1980s.

Mike Barr's remarkably diverse experiences nurtured his natural empathy, his inherited gift for bringing out the best in people of all kinds and cultures. They set him on the path to his true calling: teaching the art of persuasive communication to aspiring business leaders in the United States.

From the instant you meet Mike Barr, you sense that here is a man who could talk the gloomiest pessimist into conceding that life might actually be worth living.

If you really want to help this world,
what you will have to do is teach how to live in it.
—JOSEPH CAMPBELL

I first met Mike at the end of an out-of-town, brain-dead day when I could not wait to finish up, pack my bags, and go home to sanity. You know those days: all the meetings you thought were important just didn't pan out.

Exhausted, I still had one last meeting on my list. I knew it would be a waste of time. I went only because I had promised a friend.

Have you ever noticed how, in business and in life, just when you think all your effort has been a colossal waste, fate often reshuffles the deck and deals you a winning hand? It's a corollary to what I call "the law of first meetings": their importance will be inversely proportional to what you expect.

Mike and I had a drink at a business club in New York. Within minutes we connected. I knew immediately that we shared the same values. He understood that life depends on far more than a paycheck (although he didn't discount the value of the paycheck, either).

"I know that making a living and making a life are usually seen as separate," he began. "What I do is help my clients look carefully at their lives, at their life stories, and then ask them to align that life with how they make a living. The better they live, the better they will be at making a living."

The voice is a window on the soul.
—GERALD DE NERVAL

These eloquent words were not those of simply a "communications coach," as Mike has been described. They were the feelings of a man who has experienced life deeply and wants to share all he has learned. An Ethiopian proverb came to mind: "When the heart overflows, it comes out through the mouth."

As Mike spoke, he actually vibrated—almost as if his body were a tuning fork. He is so involved with his work and so enthusiastic about every client's possibilities that he literally breathes it. That's because his work comes from deep inside him. He infuses his work with his spirit, binding his self with your self.

I refer to Mike Barr as a "grandma." It is an honorific I reserve for those rare individuals who have developed a singular understanding not only of who they are, but those around them and how all interconnect. Children well know the power of grandmas. "The best place to be when you're sad," one little girl told me, "is Grandma's lap."

The real voyage is not in seeking new landscapes, but in seeing with new eyes and through the eyes of others.
—ANONYMOUS

Having been raised in an environment that taught only one way to live, I had my eyes opened to the incredible variety of human lives and livelihoods during the years I spent back-packing around the world after college. Yet I was amazed that, amid this diversity, there was a remarkable similarity in dreams and desires. The farmer in Bangladesh and the temporary occupant of the White House have more in common than I ever imagined.

Traveling the world and meeting its people was my school for spiritual discovery. It was during that time that I first sensed the power bestowed by a heightened awareness of those around us. I learned how to navigate through different cultures, sometimes in dangerous situations, by listening to the "grandmas," who were intimately familiar with both the fabric of a community and the threads that held it in place.

In tribal cultures grandmothers often raise the children while the parents work, and they carry the tribe's life wisdom. The grandmother concept also operates in the tribal culture of capitalism, as I later discovered. To make a sale, prevail in a negotiation, or move up the corporate ladder, it is essential to understand the motivations and power of a certain secretary, the confidence given to a particular adviser, or the influence of the keeper of an organization's cultural values.

In business parlance it might be called "understanding organizational buying behavior and the decision-making unit" or, more broadly, the "politics of a company's culture and decision making."

I like to call it "seeking common ground for uncommon results." Simply put, to succeed in today's global business world we need to understand its practices and how to achieve our objectives while respecting the perspective of others—just as Mike's parents respected the customs of numerous towns and villages in order to survive Hitler.

A wise man does not contend. Therefore, no one can contend against him. Yield and overcome.
—LAO-TZU

Mike's days are enriched by family: his wife, Janice, whom he married on the Fourth of July 1982; his four children; his brother; his sister; and his parents, Itzhak and Lola.

As both the son of Holocaust survivors and kin to the 170 members of his family who did not survive the depravity of Adolf Hitler's Germany, Mike's nights are haunted by loved ones he never met. And telling Itzhak and Lola's story became important to him when he realized that more than a few people alive today question whether the Holocaust actually occurred—"not because they're evil or malicious, but because they just don't know."

So Mike devoted himself to understanding his parents' survival, and, in telling their story, he found that his sense of what to do with his own life became clear. As in the old English saying, "A good example is the best sermon," Mike came to recognize the importance of connecting with people starkly different from himself. He saw that for his parents— strangers in a strange land—sensitivity to the dialects, customs, and dress of others was self-preservation.

"Because they were so flexible," Mike told me, "they were able to align themselves with whatever was going on each day in whatever community they passed through. And because they understood the big picture facing those people—and communicated their understanding—they were able to move safely from one community to another, like fishermen stepping from stone to stone across a roaring stream."

Mike never forgets that he owes his life and its blessings to his parents' courage, strength, faith, and adaptability. Nor does he ever forget—although he can barely speak of it— that those of his parents' generation who were unable to adapt were extinguished.

The son of Itzhak and Lola has adapted his life from their lives, creating two stories about the magic power words play in winning over people. Not that the stories are of equal weight, as he acknowledges. "For my parents, language was a camouflage for survival; for me, it is the foundation of my living."

Mike Barr's workdays are consumed by a diverse cross section of business executives who enlist his help to improve their leadership skills.

First they came for the socialists, and I did not speak out because I was not a socialist. Then they came for the trade unionists, and I did not speak out because I was not a trade unionist. Then they came for the Jews, and I did not speak out because I was not a Jew. Then they came for me, and there was no one left to speak for me.
—MARTIN NIEMÖLLER

Mike's parents grew up together in Lvov in the Ukraine, on the border between Poland and what was then the Soviet Union. They learned to speak Polish, Ukrainian, German, and Russian and studied French in school. Yiddish was their first language, with Hebrew for worship.

Both families lived for generations in a part of the world where new rulers came and went—the Hapsburgs of Austria, the Poles, the Bolsheviks. It meant you kept your ears open to changing sounds and your mind open to changing possibilities. Your real home was inside yourself.

In 1941 Hitler's troops streamed across the Polish border to invade Russia. For the Jews of Lvov it was a death sentence. Lifetime friends turned Jews over to the authorities. Mike's parents and their families were herded into a nearby labor camp. For those who survived its brutality, the next stop was Auschwitz.

Realizing that their only hope for survival lay in escape, Mike's parents climbed the fence one night and ran east, dodging the guards' bullets. The labor camp commandant didn't even bother to send soldiers after the two teenagers.

After all, he reasoned, they were Jews; they would quickly be picked up by Ukrainian locals and turned over to Nazi authorities.

Courage is rightly esteemed the first of human qualities because it is the quality which guarantees all others.
—WINSTON CHURCHILL

Only if the young couple could pass for locals wherever they went might they have a chance. But the slightest trace of a Yiddish accent would give them away—and mean certain death.

Also, every Ukrainian village had its own dialect. The young couple slept in the fields, and when the village girls came through the fields at dawn to get water from the well, they listened carefully. They noted the dialect, marked the style of banter, and absorbed the inflections of conversation. They copied their dress, their hairstyles.

And so they went from town to town, talking with people in their own language and dialect, emulating their style and manner, persuading them that they were just a couple of Ukrainian teenagers on the move.

They were well into Russia when they were suddenly stopped by a group of Russian soldiers. When the soldiers heard their story, they didn't believe it. "Impossible. No one could have walked here from Lvov," they said. "The land between us is held by Nazi armored columns. You must be lying. You are spies!"

Ironically, having reached what should have been safety, the pair was on the verge of being shot. At the last possible moment, Itzhak turned to the colonel, pleading: "Do you have someone who speaks Yiddish?"

A Yiddish-speaking Russian soldier appeared. After some

conversation he realized they were telling the truth: this boy and girl were not spies; they were Jews.

Itzhak and Lola would learn after Hitler's defeat that they were among the few in either of their families to survive.

We are governed not by armies and police, but by ideas.
—MONA CAIRD

The young couple settled briefly in France, where Mike was born in 1948, but then moved to a new country, Israel.

"I witnessed in my early years this fledgling state fighting a war for its own survival," Mike recalls. "There, my father juggled several jobs at the university and in the Israeli government, persuading new refugees to plunge into building Israel in the midst of war."

Itzhak was so successful that in 1957 the government sent the family to live in Mexico City, a base from which Itzhak promoted Israel throughout Latin America. Speaking to Jewish communities all over the region, Itzhak urged them to raise money for Israel and to settle there as well. Mike often accompanied his father on these tours.

"My father traveled to almost every little town in Latin America where there was a Jewish community . . . from Santo Domingo to Mexico to Argentina. He spoke right before the synagogue services began. He would speak in Spanish, lacing his presentations with words in Hebrew, Yiddish, Polish, whatever the congregation spoke, telling them of the Israeli government's work with refugees in Israel and about the war.

"I would watch as he reduced his audience to tears and inspired them to action. I marveled at his ability to speak so persuasively and, at the same time, with such tremendous urgency. I was so proud of him, of his ability to blend his idealism—unbroken by Hitler or anybody else—with a practical need to build a country, and of his ability to create bridges to any audience."

Even today when Mike describes his father's commanding presence, his lightly accented speech flows in a deep baritone and his eyes well up. "That's when I began my career," he says. "I was so excited by the idea that you could use speech to motivate, to sell, to teach. And I was fascinated by the idea of melding one's work with one's life as he did."

> **Don't wait to make your son a great man.**
> **Make him a great boy.**
> —RUSSIAN SAYING

By the time Mike was fifteen, he had lived in Cuba as Castro came to power, and then, as the Kennedy years began, he and his family moved to the heartland of the United States: Kansas. Master of four languages, he adored his father, who was becoming more of an academic, a teacher renowned for his mastery of language and history.

In the United States Mike was a cultural sponge. "I arrived at the time of Camelot, when American idealism was speaking to the world, trying to persuade the world of values I shared deeply. The United States was communicating—through the Peace Corps, foreign aid—that it wanted to give something back to the world."

The United States also struck Mike as "an amazing melting pot." And for his family, which had lived in so many places and whose experiences had been so intimately connected with uniting refugees from many lands into a single nation, a melting pot was an entirely comfortable milieu.

"People thought of us as being so different," Mike remembers. "They would constantly ask me about my experiences. 'What was it like?' they wanted to know. So I learned to tell the story of where I had been, what I had learned, the dangers I feared, the hopes I felt."

The late 1960s found the family moving around Canada—another different culture—as Itzhak, now a professor of Spanish literature, climbed the academic ladder. Mike finished college there and then set off to get his master's degree in comparative literature at Harvard, a natural for him.

But Mike felt guilty about his lack of military service, so he returned to Israel to serve his army duty. He arrived in time for the Yom Kippur War.

Citing his language ability, he tried to get into intelligence work. But the Israeli defense force included former taxi drivers and handymen who spoke sixteen languages because, as an officer told Mike, "they had to." Instead Mike was assigned to an armored engineering unit.

"I saw how you take kids who have emigrated from all over the world—Russians, Ethiopians, Argentines—and you turn them into soldiers. It's an incredible transformation. These are some of the proudest soldiers in the world, and they're proud because they've learned the story of their people, their nation, their own roles in their nation's defense."

The time had come for Mike to return to his new home, the United States, to take up teaching. But a chance event would change his life.

> **A musician must make his music,**
> **an artist must paint, a poet must write,**
> **if he is to ultimately be at peace with himself.**
> —ABRAHAM MASLOW

Mike tried academia for two and a half years, teaching literature at Brooklyn College at the start of its open admissions policy.

"They were bringing in kids from all over, trying to get

them up to speed. Since I spoke so many of the languages, I was given the task of trying to convince the kids that a college education was worth working hard at. That was tougher—and more important—than teaching them literature."

Mike found this teaching fulfilling, but he became restless. Looking for a different kind of challenge, he became a consultant for the training and development department at Bankers Trust Corporation in New York. It was 1977. The entire banking system was undergoing radical changes in the form of global competition and technological transformation.

Mike's challenge was to train many of the bank's foreign employees, from Hong Kong to Moscow, to become more articulate about the systems that they were helping to implement in the transformation of the bank. He was still a teacher.

This might have been his career at Bankers Trust for years to come if not for a chance encounter in a hallway with the assistant to the chairman. This man was preparing to usher in a culture change that would fundamentally remake Bankers Trust: the phasing out of retail banking to focus on investment banking.

He began by asking, "Do you know anything about banking?" Mike shook his head to indicate that he didn't and began walking away. "Wonderful," the man said, "I want to work with you."

Mike was shocked, but not for long. It was his turn to "go to school."

"At the time, I didn't even realize what a consultant was," Mike recalls. "I got a quick lesson with that first assignment. We had to persuade the bank's concerned, and often outraged, investors all over the world that this strategy was right, that the bank—and their investment in the bank— would not be harmed by the change but would actually benefit."

**From here that looks like a bucket of water,
but from an ant's point of view, it's a vast ocean;
from an elephant's point of view, just a cool drink;
and to a fish, of course, it's home.**
—*THE PHANTOM TOLL BOOTH*

Mike did what came naturally to him. He didn't just help craft the message; he role-played with hostile audiences, promised them total confidentiality, and received honest feedback from different constituencies with differing perspectives.

"I am often a mirror," he explains. "What looks in, looks out." His father would be proud.

Soon Mike Barr became Barr Associates. His company grew over the next two decades as he learned to market himself and his services—something initially alien to this teacher-turned-consultant.

"I thought it was like academia," Mike says. "You come in, you train the students, and that's it. Then somebody at the bank turned to me and said, 'You actually have to market yourself.' 'What's that?' I asked. 'That's what you do,' he said. 'You're a persuader. Now persuade us that we need you.'"

So Mike got a quick lesson in consultative selling. It developed into a career in executive development consulting, focusing on the art and the skills of persuasion by understanding others first, then yourself. Before long he was selling those skills to dozens of other companies.

Since its debut twenty-one years ago, Barr Associates has worked with over thirty large global corporations and dozens of smaller ones. The firm, whose clients include Merrill Lynch & Company and Johnson & Johnson, concentrates on the finance and health care industries. What exactly does Barr Associates do?

Mike says it best: "Barr Associates helps driven executives transform themselves into statesmen. They must discern how they are perceived by others inside and outside the company and become more profoundly aware of bigger issues than just getting the job done, advancing their careers, and making money. Statesmen realize that to really be successful, they must understand and communicate how we are all part of a bigger story."

One ongoing eleven-year relationship provides a taste of how Mike and Barr Associates goes beyond merely helping executives communicate better, to helping them change their own lives and the lives of those around them. The result is more humane executives and more humane companies.

> **You will derive your supreme satisfaction . . .**
> **from your ability to identify yourselves with others**
> **and to share fully in their needs and hopes.**
> —NORMAN COUSINS

In 1988 Mike was called into the largest health care corporation in the world to help the president of one of their companies respond to feedback received from his own employees in the biannual internal survey.

He was a seasoned executive but had been with this particular company for only a year. Traditionalists grumbled that this man did not understand how things were done at the company, and his change initiatives, though effective strategically, had some of the employees in an uproar.

Viewing himself as "an extremely good communicator," but bowing to board pressure nonetheless, the executive agreed to meet with Mike for five minutes, "as a courtesy." To keep the meeting short and uncomfortable, he met with Mike in a basement room.

Mike entered, and after barely a hello, he confronted the executive: "I heard from some of your people that you read your mail when you speak to your employees. They feel insulted."

"Well, that goes to show you! They just don't understand how my efficiency benefits them. I can do both—and well," the president retorted gruffly.

Mike did not back down: "Many agree with you that there's a need for change. They just resent the symbols—the way you are doing it. Remember that it's not what you say, but how people perceive what you say." Mike won over a new client.

Over the next several years Mike shadowed the president, surveyed key decision makers within the company, and then coached his client on the totality of his image. Specialists were brought in as needed to make sure that what the president said was in alignment with his personal goals as well as with the goals of the company and all his constituents.

Barr Associates eventually worked with all the members of the health care company's board and with several other executives. But the most satisfying result was the growth and transformation of the president himself into a powerful and highly respected statesman.

**Change is a door
that can only be opened from the inside.**
—TERRY NEIL

"Whenever we begin," Mike acknowledges, "much of the work is mechanical—practicing a speech, working with certain words and language, and body postures. We use a lot of videotape and begin to craft an external image. Here, I was dealing with someone who wanted to say to his employees, 'Why should I work so hard to convince you? Waste of our time. You know perfectly well that I know what to do in this marketplace. Just do what I say!'

"Then we progress to aligning everything he does with the changing needs of the company. We create more opportunities for him to speak to and interact with his employees. Here is where the internal, personal changes begin.

"He slowly becomes more comfortable being with his people, talking and listening to them. Then people begin buying into his vision, and he himself starts creating more opportunities to be with his people, as he begins to enjoy them as more than just employees. They now are associates traveling on the same path of trying to do something special together. They have found a common ground.

"At this point, his entire leadership style has begun to change from 'I' to 'we.' As Martin Buber would say, he is moving from an 'I-It' set of relationships to an 'I-Thou.' The isolated gunslinger atop the hierarchy, struggling to get his people to buy in, is now communicating effectively his vision."

When this leader eventually realized that his real goal was "to improve the way we take care of ourselves," Mike says, he left the health care provider to join a venture capital company that focuses on the most revolutionary segment of the industry: genetics. Today he is one of the leading venture capitalists, with several companies, many of which Barr Associates services.

Mike remains a very important part of this executive's informal brain trust. He acts as a regular sounding board and an objective voice, providing feedback on how the executive is perceived by others and how effective he is in communicating with them.

Mike observes: "He used to be focused on competition and excellence. Now he is more humane. Even with his children, he doesn't push the same. It's more 'Do what you love.' He has gone from an executive who, when faced with the AIDS crisis in Africa, would retort, 'How are we going to make any money on that?' to a person whose reaction is tears of empathy."

**Jazz comes from who you are, where you've been,
what you've done. If you don't live it,
it won't come out of your horn.**
—CHARLIE PARKER

How to describe Mike at work . . . I'll use a story about an incident at an executive retreat.

Four executives are out running one morning when they come upon a "No Trespassing" sign in the woods.

"Let's go," says the CEO. The second executive says, "No, I can't break the law." The third suggests, "Let's go in, look around for any people, and if we don't see anyone, proceed." Finally, the last one offers, "Let's first just scope out the situation, and then we can decide."

What if Mike Barr had been among the group? He would have commanded, "First, let's blow up the sign. Then let's stop for a moment, breathe deeply this wonderful air, thank God for his beautiful day, and then let's go."

Mike's work is the air he breathes. He once told me that the word *breath* and the word *spirit* are the same in several languages.

So it will come as no surprise when I tell you that he also cares. He affirms the saying "People are more influenced by how much you care than how much you know." Caring is essential to his effectiveness, to the trust he nurtures in each of his clients.

When Mike Barr works with you, you sense that he exudes caring, and you are changed.

**To get into the core of God at his greatest,
one must first get into the core of himself at his least.**
—JOHANNES ECKHART

What Mike does, quite simply, is strip you down to your heart and soul. He gets rid of the masks and peels back all those accumulated layers of corporate "stuff"—adult stuff— to help you communicate from deep inside . . . heart to heart, soul to soul.

Soon you sound so real, so honest, that people hug you, love you, and, hopefully, follow you.

How does he do it? With deep psychoanalysis? Not exactly. By talking you out of your shell? Not really. By listening to your stories? That's part of it. What, then? As Charles Churchill observed, "Those who would make us feel must feel themselves."

Mike gets naked and stays naked. In front of a group of executives on their first day with him, he will talk about his own inner demons—the ghosts that haunt his dreams. After that, the executives can speak only from their hearts or they will sound false.

The real work can now begin.

He makes you feel safe, but uncomfortable. He opens himself up so completely, so honestly, so deeply, giving all he has through his entire being, that he leaves you no choice: join him, because he won't stop until you sign up.

Unless you tell him to stop, that is. He changes the lives only of those who want to change—of those who will relate from the personal "I," not the corporate "we." He wants to help you humanize your business life and the life within your organization.

"I serve as something of a rehearsal studio," Mike says, "a safe place for people to let go, try things out, take a risk, experiment with ideas—and get feedback. Here they rehearse the words that can appeal to different constituencies in different situations, sometimes in different cultures, for different purposes.

"In this safe space, people grow by experimenting— something that has become less and less possible in today's highly competitive, often risk-averse business world. How else can people or organizations grow?"

Executives know that to be unique and valued in today's business environment, they have to be different in a way that resonates with people. Values are what set you apart, but feeling comfortable expressing them, and knowing how to communicate them to different audiences in different settings, requires the talents of a Mike Barr.

If you are coming to help me, you are wasting your time.
But if you are coming because your liberation
is bound up with mine, then let us work together.
—AUSTRALIAN ABORIGINAL WOMAN

Mike has been successful because he is hooked on the elixir of service. He must work, he says, because like any addict, he has to have his fix. And his fix is your fix, so to speak. He wants, and needs, that rush every day.

Mike is what he does. He communicates from the heart, relating stories in a staccato style, one after the other. The truth of the world, of our lives, and of his life comes through in these stories—stories that reveal who we are and why we are, allowing no one to hide.

For Mike Barr, the power of persuasive communication—of finding a common ground among different constituencies—is no abstraction, and the purpose of work is not just to make a living.

"In my work," he says, "I see my whole life embodied. Some people, like Hitler, spend their lives persuading have-nots to seek 'justice' by committing terrible evils. Others strive for the exact opposite—persuading have-nots to build a future where there is work, meaning, hope.

"People can talk their way to a Holocaust, and they can talk their way to creating the Peace Corps, building a Microsoft, or declaring war on poverty. I've seen both. I've seen people communicate by blowing each other's houses down, and I've seen them communicate through goodness.

"I'm trying to use everything I have to teach business-people that it is okay to talk about a personal component in business. It's not romantic. It's not impractical. It's the only hope for mankind.

"My parents cowered in the fields and waited to see what kind of language was spoken so they could survive. We all have to learn to speak the language of mutual understanding."

Mike Barr is one of my teachers, one of my heroes, for many reasons. Mostly, however, I feel this way because he has shown me what happens when someone gives you all he has, taking back what you want to give. It is one of the purest forms of love.

The only gift is a portion of thyself.
—RALPH WALDO EMERSON

✱

Lifelines

A friend once told me, "If you can figure out whether a four-year-old or a six-year-old should get the last piece of toffee, you can negotiate any contract." In a way, she was echoing Harry Truman when he said, "I have found that the best way to give advice to your children is to find out what they want and then advise them to do it."

How much time do you spend learning about others before trying to persuade them? Good communicators speak in the words of their audience. They understand their motivations, their unspoken needs. They create a common ground. That is how they persuade.

Communication is not a technical science, but a personal expression. It is about communicating as one person to another, revealing yourself as a personal, human "I," not hiding behind the royal, corporate "we." Being a leader today also requires an understanding of different cultures and of the power relationships within an organization, as well as an appreciation of differences in how diverse groups of people think and live.

Mike Barr's life has been built on these principles. They meant survival for his parents. They are a life and a living for him.

Man masters nature not by force, but by understanding.
—JACOB BRONOWSKI

CHAPTER 9

✴

FIND OUT WHERE YOU FIT IN BY NOT FITTING IN

Katie Paine's Stepping-Stones

**The gem cannot be polished without friction,
nor man perfected without trial.**
—CONFUCIUS

Fitting in life can be a lonely business. Fitting rooms tend to be for one person at a time. You can come out and ask the sales clerk or your friends what they think, but even if they're telling the truth, it's their truth.
—Noah ben Shea

The room fell silent.

Standing at the front of the classroom, I wasn't sure what to do next. My eyes and heart were locked with his in one of those rare moments of truth that come in a flash but remain with you always.

Should I make eye contact with the other seventy students who just heard what I heard? Should I say something? Should I wait until one of them had the courage to respond to the power of his words?

To gain some perspective on what was happening in my classroom, imagine a West Point cadet standing up in a class on infantry warfare, taking a deep breath, and then eloquently declaring himself a pacifist. Even more extraordinary, imagine his fellow cadets listening in stunned silence and then giving him an ovation. Could anything be more incongruous in a roomful of future generals?

The setting was Stanford Business School, not West Point, and the room was filled with future chief executives, not army generals. But what had just happened was virtually identical.

During my seminar on humanistic values in business, a brave student took a chance and opened up. He spoke from the heart, and his words defied the perceived cultural values of Stanford and shattered the protocol of its classrooms.

Though we were surprised by his words, it was evident

that we all understood what he was saying and what he felt. We had not only been there, but, in many respects, had yet to leave. You just weren't supposed to say these things in a class.

> My great religion is a belief in the blood,
> the flesh, as being wiser than the intellect.
> We can go wrong in our minds. But what
> our blood feels and believes and says is always true.
> —D. H. LAWRENCE

This young man—I'll call him Jim—described how he came from one of America's poorest urban areas. He worked hard—supported emotionally by parents trying just to "get by"—and made it to an Ivy League college. He did well and, upon graduation, secured an analyst's job at a top investment bank. Working on big deals with high-level clientele, he was soon making over $75,000 a year.

Jim's parents were understandably proud. It was expected that after a few years he would go to a top business school, get his MBA, and return to investment banking. By all of society's external measures he was a success, winning big time on the proverbial fast track.

But there was another Jim, one who was struggling with values, and this Jim, by his own internal measures, was falling apart. During his last year at work he spent part of every day crying in a stall in the corporate bathroom.

The other class members and I stared in silence, afraid to meet anyone else's eyes, as he described all this.

Jim told us how torn he was between what he was doing and who he felt he really was. The solution he finally came up with was to go to business school. He had somehow hoped that business school would be his ticket out. But Stanford was merely dragging him in deeper.

179

The business school culture was all about $100,000 starting salaries, high-profile Silicon Valley jobs, and career opportunities that only MBAs from top schools are lucky enough to get. Would he be strong enough this time to resist the temptations, to go the more difficult route in order to stay true to himself?

Tears welled up in Jim's eyes and his voice cracked as he fought his way through his story.

The whole class listened as one, intent on his every word—not because he was saying anything new (such doubts haunt businesspeople at all levels), but because he had the courage to say it out loud in an elite classroom.

Here was a student who was sharing feelings of loneliness and a sense of "What am I doing here?" that are seldom revealed publicly. In fact, most business schools and corporate cultures consider them unacceptable, if not outright shameful.

Yet instead of derisive laughter or sneering indifference to Jim's candor, this community of students embraced him. Many came up to talk to him after class. Some hugged him.

In more than twenty years of teaching highly ambitious MBA candidates, I had never experienced an epiphany like this. Jim had broken the unspoken rules, and this day his peers responded with compassion. It was an overwhelming outpouring of love.

I'm delighted to report that Jim did indeed resist the external pressure. He graduated Stanford well equipped in mind and spirit to pursue what was right for him—a public service career in his urban neighborhood that urgently needed everything he had to give.

(I'm also happy to report that this path has become more common as the millennium approaches. More business school students are following Jim's lead.)

So Jim is not the only one who is better off because he rejected what for him would have been a hollow life. Our world is better off, too.

FIND OUT WHERE YOU FIT IN BY NOT FITTING IN

When I was much younger, I kept trying to fit in and people kept pushing me away. They kept telling me I just didn't fit in. Soon, so many people kept pushing me away, I found I had a perspective.
—BUCKMINSTER FULLER

Finding where you fit in is seldom a fairy tale of luck, love, money, and grandeur. More often it involves pain, soul-searching, and mistakes. The process is as much a matter of figuring out who we are not as it is one of determining who we are. It is something we all must go through if we want to make a life and make a living.

If we do it, if we kiss enough frogs along the way, we'll be able to recognize our prince when he comes along, because by then we will truly know ourselves. We just have to have the courage to follow up by saying aloud who we are, acting on it, and sustaining it.

Katharine Delahaye Paine—"Katie" to her legion of friends—is an avid sailor, aspiring writer, and successful entrepreneur who knows all about the pitfalls of self-discovery. Katie's life journey, on the way to founding the Delahaye Group—her own $5 million, image and reputation measurement firm—was a series of zigs and zags. But as we know, the shortest route between two life points is seldom a straight one.

Katie's life turned away from the promising journalism career her admiring parents originally envisioned for her, but for years it still continued along an acceptable path. For much of her life that path fulfilled what Katie believed were her dreams—until the day she finally asked herself, "Whose dream is this, anyway?"

That's a question Katie still isn't sure she's answered. Although today she's busy opening offices in Asia, Europe, and Latin America, selling her brand of "business with a soul," tomorrow she may be on a postponed sailing trip around the world or running for political office. Or maybe she will return to one of her early loves—writing—replacing business reports with books.

**A happy life is one which is in accordance
with its own nature.**
—LUCIUS ANNAEUS SENECA

"Didn't everybody grow up in a house that had a living room coffee table with at least fifty magazines, the last twelve issues of every magazine published?" So it once seemed to Katie Paine, the only child of the publisher of *Fortune* magazine.

Del Paine was forty-six years old when Katie was born in 1952. Katie's mother, the editor of *Harper's Bazaar,* also had a daughter from a previous marriage who was thirteen years older than Katie. When her half-sister married a doctor and produced three children, "the message was clear," says Katie. "Get married. Have children. Don't work."

But the examples of her parents and her closeness to her father sent a different set of signals. "My life model was more like the men in a family," Katie realizes. "I was asked how I was going to make my mark on the world."

At the Paines' elegant brownstone on Manhattan's Upper East Side and their summer home in New Hampshire, Daddy's little girl was introduced early to famous dinner guests such as Henry Luce, the founder of *Time* and *Life* magazines, and his wife, Clare Booth Luce, playwright and diplomat. Even Katie's aunt and uncle were well-known magazine editors. You can imagine the dinner table conversation in this glittering circle.

Katie would, of course, be a writer herself someday. It was preordained when your "whole world was writers and journalists." (Among the list of regular houseguests, Katie knew but one doctor and no lawyers.) She had no idea there was anything else to do in life besides observing, reporting, analyzing, and interpreting the events of our time in newspapers, magazines, and books.

**One learns through the heart,
not the eyes or the intellect.**
—MARK TWAIN

Katie's childhood wasn't all sweetness, however. Her parents had a professional marriage; they kissed once a year, on Christmas. Her mother traveled constantly for *Harper's Bazaar,* often spending weeks in Europe for the summer collections.

It was during the summers that Katie and her dad left the city for New Hampshire. He worked little, devoting long country days to his precious daughter. It was their special time together, before the changing leaves of fall beckoned their return to New York, bringing a little heartbreak for a daughter.

When Katie was nineteen her father took her around the world. She cherished him, "though I did everything he didn't want. I was a typical rebellious teenager. Dad's friends were all conservatives. I wasn't."

Katie returned from the trip to go to Connecticut College, study Indian history, and emerge determined to be a magazine editor like her parents. Instead she fell in love with Doug Chapin. Three years younger than Katie, Doug was a premed student at Johns Hopkins University in Baltimore.

After college Katie put her ambitions on the back burner and moved to Maryland to live with Doug. She recalls those ensuing years of trying to find her place, her fit: "'Thou shalt know what thou wants to be when thou grows up' is not the Eleventh Commandment."

**Perfection is finally attained not when
there is no longer anything to add, but when
there is no longer anything to take away.**
—ANTOINE DE SAINT-EXUPÉRY

Though Katie yearned to be a photojournalist, she started her predestined career "on the newspaper side of it," as an editor for a suburban Maryland paper and a copy aide at *The Washington Post.*

"Part of it was fun. When you're twenty-three, going to receptions for Golda Meir or George Meany is cool. But most of it wasn't cool. At the *Post* I was just following a photographer, taking names of the people he photographed. I wasn't writing. It wasn't what I wanted to do, and I wasn't very patient," Katie reflects.

When Doug decided he didn't want to be a doctor after all, they moved to New Hampshire. Katie grew restless. "I wasn't so sure about this whole career thing anyway. I wanted to get married and have a family."

But a family friend arranged a job on the *Boston Herald.* Katie's mother made the introduction. "Mr. Hearst, may I present my daughter, Katie," she began. "Katie wants to be a journalist, Mr. Hearst."

"Don't think talent has anything to do with this 'getting ahead,'" remarks Katie, who was so startled by the introduction that she dropped a cucumber on his foot.

"They gave me a job I hated. It was totally irrelevant. I wasn't saving the world. I wasn't doing anything meaningful. And again, I wasn't writing." She applied for every other job she might possibly qualify for, on the *Herald* and anywhere else. No luck.

Three months later Hearst brought in a new editor for the Sunday magazine, Geoffrey Precourt. His dad had worked for Del Paine. Katie finally browbeat Precourt into hiring her for the team assigned to refurbish the magazine, and "Geoffrey turned me into a journalist," Katie acknowledges.

"He took me under his wing and said, 'This is how to write a sentence, and this is how to put dancing girls in the headlines, and this is how to get people to pay attention to what you write.' Literally, he taught me how to write. He was the mentor I needed."

> **I am a great believer in luck, and I find that**
> **the harder I work, the more I have of it.**
> —THOMAS JEFFERSON

"Today, thousands of protesters gathered at the gates of the Seabrook nuclear power plant to protest what has become New Hampshire's biggest question," began the *Herald*'s April 1, 1977, lead story, bylined "Katharine D. Paine."

"I was lucky. It must have been predestined," Katie says when recalling how her "big break" finally came about.

"I was in there with the other 1,400 protesters (all of whom were arrested), getting to know the Clamshell Alliance [her future source of inside information on all the nuclear protests], when I had to run out to call in to the paper. While I was out, the arrests began. I couldn't get back in. Instead, I had breaking news."

Her dad was thrilled. He loved the byline, if not the politics. He clipped all the articles, reserved extra newspaper copies.

Covering Seabrook led to Katie's prominence as not only the Seabrook expert, but also as a force in New Hampshire politics—television networks called Katie for the inside scoop. Other offers to write and edit began to materialize.

Katie took one: copy editor for the gossip page of the *Herald*'s daily paper. The hours were great, it was an easy job, and she was the editor, not an assistant. But not for long: the job was neither meaningful nor challenging, and a harassing boss didn't make things any better.

So when a reporter's job on the city desk opened up, Katie went after it. She began reporting on trends, which was simply "calling three people who agree about something and you've got a trend." Katie Paine was having fun.

Grassroots work helped her identify important trends— the kind that pointed to newsworthy tidbits like who would be the next governor. She hung around enough places and talked to enough people to know that "people were becoming less concerned with Pop Warner football and turning to soccer." It was a shift that signaled changes in people's politics as well.

In 1978 New Hampshire's powerful politico Mel Thompson was expected to anoint his son, Peter, as the next governor. But "Seabrook was going to be a big issue," Katie recalls, "and the crown prince was totally out of touch."

CBS said Peter Thompson would win easily. Katharine D. Paine said Hugh Gallen "will give him a run for his money." The night of the election, she predicted Gallen's victory. He won.

"That damn Boston media," groused Mel Thompson. Katie smiled.

**We could never learn to be brave and patient
if there were only joy in the world.**
—HELEN KELLER

The day after the election Katie followed Doug to Santa Cruz, California, where he was now studying physics and economics. She worked as a stringer for the *San Francisco Chronicle,* then as a temporary employee writing for the *San Jose Mercury.* Her first piece was "Theft of Computer Chips: Chips for Coke."

Working for a daily meant crazy hours, writing lots of copy—an entire front page each day. In 1979 Katie and Doug married, but "all I was doing was working. I never saw Doug. I didn't even get time off to go to my cousin's wedding.

"Then I applied for a bureau job on the *Mercury* in Palo Alto. I really wanted this job. The editors had sought me out. They wanted me to apply for the job, and then they didn't give it to me. I was devastated. It changed my life."

Backed by the union, Katie filed a grievance. Newspaper Guild rules say that a job must be offered first to a qualified temporary employee before it can be offered to someone from outside the newspaper.

Upside down. It turned the world she thought she knew, the world she thought she fit into, on its head. "It tore me apart," Katie admits.

"A grievance hearing is the worst thing in the world. You can't defend yourself," says Katie. "Here I am, Daddy's little girl who could do no wrong, who has gotten only praise all her life for her wonderful writing, and this grievance hearing absolutely destroyed my credibility.

"These were my work friends. I had to listen to eight hours of 'You can't write, you can't edit, you're not qualified for the job.' And you can't defend yourself! I had no opportunity to argue back."

**We all have big changes in our lives
that are more or less a second chance.**
—HARRISON FORD

"Everything that Daddy promised wasn't going to come true," Katie realized. "Just because he said I could always do anything I put my mind to, anything I worked hard at, it didn't necessarily mean that I'd get my way all the time. Or that things would be fair.

"I wanted everything delivered to me right then—without gaining the experience, without showing the patience. All my life I heard, 'You'll never have any trouble getting a job in the newspaper business.' It wasn't happening that way."

Katie was out, but she didn't know anything else. She had no other expectations, no other frame of reference. She had taken a few graphic arts courses, mostly to know more about newspaper design and layout, and had enjoyed them.

Ever since her wedding Katie felt that she should be home to cook dinner—as Doug's mother and sisters did. They all had a more "normal" life, quitting work once they married. As it happened, the timing was right. Katie also wanted more time at home with Doug. Or so she thought. So she looked for something different, something in corporate America. After all, in 1980 journalists thought corporate America meant working normal hours.

Her corporate experience, coupled with her earlier grass-roots work, would turn out to be a training ground for starting her own company seven years down the road.

There are no wrong turns,
only wrong thinking on the turns our life has taken.
—ZEN SAYING

"Advertising Coordinator," read the ad in the *San Jose Mercury.* "Knowledge of the English language helpful." The ad was from the microwave radio division of a small engineering firm, Harris-Farinon.

Katie knew nothing about microwave radios, nothing about engineering, and nothing about marketing. She got the job.

At Harris-Farinon Katie wrote press releases, managed the customer information systems, set up a measurement system for advertising evaluation, prepared for trade shows, wrote brochures and data sheets—just about everything short of trade and media advertising.

But that wasn't the hard part.

The hard part was having to tell friends and family that she was no longer an exalted journalist and was now a "lowly publicist." The hard part was confounding all those long-standing expectations. And dealing with issues of self-image.

After years of total understanding from her father, "all of a sudden I'm working for a company, an industry, he's never heard of. I'm three thousand miles away, and he doesn't have a clue to what I'm doing every day. And my friends in journalism don't understand it, either."

It was 1980. It was high tech (not then the household term it has since become). Katie Paine was working in a place that seemed to be more about dreams than reality. A place that was just beginning to be called "Silicon Valley." As she recalls, "There wasn't even traffic yet."

She liked it. She was learning, the money was good, and she had a good boss. Katie was close to home, working nine to five, playing soccer and sailing, making new friends. It made sense.

What's more, Doug was happy at Pacific Gas & Electric, and the marriage seemed to be going well.

Paradise, right? Wrong. After two years Katie was bored: "I'm doing the same thing. I'm not challenged. I need something else."

In Silicon Valley in the 1980s, that was the signal to change jobs. Katie's thirtieth birthday was at hand—as was the beginning of the end of her marriage.

> **The cure for boredom is curiosity.**
> **There is no cure for curiosity.**
> —ELLEN PARR

Katie began to realize that she always became restless each fall. This was her second fall at Harris-Farinon, and she wanted something new and challenging. She wasn't growing, she wasn't learning.

Doug moved on to Hewlett-Packard. With her strong Silicon Valley qualifications, Katie went after three jobs and took the one that offered the most money—marketing communications manager at Fujitsu.

She had a great boss, great colleagues, "the biggest loose budget in the Valley," and big authority to do important, creative things. Katie hired a new agency whose directors taught her all about integrated communications. The work was great, and she was having fun again.

At a time when the word *chip* meant chocolate or poker to most people, Katie—always the reporter—understood the tremendous potential of this new technology. She sensed intuitively "where it was going and how fast it was going to get there."

Meanwhile she and Doug were living the legendary life of Silicon Valley yuppies: the BMWs, the big house, masters of the Cuisinart. They had it all.

But having it all can have its drawbacks. Katie's hours lengthened, with twelve-hour days the minimum. "In Silicon Valley, you play with people you work with, work with people you play with," Katie says.

Fate would play a deciding role. When her marketing director committed suicide, neither Katie nor the company ever fully recovered.

The semiconductor industry went into a downturn. Katie's job was redefined, simplified. No "new" anything. Her instructions were: "Do nothing for a year and a half."

**If we don't change our direction,
we are likely to end up where we are headed.**
—ANCIENT CHINESE PROVERB

Katie got a job at Doug's employer, Hewlett-Packard. There she worked fifteen hours a day for the next six months. "You can't work like that and expect your marriage to last," Katie reflects.

That summer she was going through a legal separation at the same time that HP was introducing their laser and ink-jet printers as well as the first laptop. There were huge marketing campaigns shaping and supporting each product launch. Suddenly the company began to feel like the army.

"There were certain things that you were expected to do," Katie remembers, "and you were supposed to be patient and not go around your boss. My boss and I weren't getting along."

She wanted to move up the corporate ladder but lacked the patience to wait for as long as it would take. She had gotten that by-now-familiar feeling of claustrophobia. It was the fall—October 10, 1984, to be exact.

Katie chose a start-up company, Leemah, in Hayward, California. Her marriage dissolved, and she started dating again, a long-distance relationship with someone on the East Coast.

The next fall a call came from Lotus Development Corporation in Boston. "We're thinking about hiring somebody from the West Coast to be head of corporate communications. Are you willing to think about moving?"

"Sure," Katie replied. She was going back.

> **In the world there are only two tragedies. One is not getting what one wants, and the other is getting it.**
> —OSCAR WILDE

Lotus was Katie's twelfth company in eleven years. This was a big change. "I moved across the country, changed jobs, got divorced, all in one year," she says. Then, when she arrived at Lotus, she made a startling discovery: "This wasn't my dream. It was my parents' dream! I, too, had been living my parents' life."

It all came home to her when someone asked her how she liked being at Lotus. She replied, almost without thinking: "This is the job I was brought up to have. This is why they sent me to the schools that they sent me to, and this is why they trained me, and this is what I was meant to do."

Katie says she "never bothered to wonder whether this is what I wanted to do or if it was something I was good at doing. I was climbing a corporate ladder. I was doing all the things I was supposed to be doing—get the raise, climb another rung of the ladder, manage a few more people, take on some more responsibilities."

The job at Lotus lasted a year.

During that year Katie was working so hard—she had one stretch of thirty-one consecutive sixteen-hour days—that she burned out. She finally realized she wasn't the corporate type and, even more important, she hated her job.

"It's clear there is a pattern here. There's got to be a better way," she decided. With each year and with each job, Katharine Delahaye Paine had narrowed the possibilities of where she would fit in.

I think of life as a good book. The further you get into it, the more it begins to make sense.
—RABBI HAROLD KUSHNER

Katie had devised a methodology for measuring the effectiveness of public relations. It was based largely on grassroots surveys and local press analysis. From that grew an idea for a consulting firm that "would operate in the gap between agencies and corporate America."

She resigned from Lotus and started her new company, the Delahaye Group, in January 1987. She didn't know how to run a company, but she learned—just as she had learned to write a headline, run a trade show, and launch an integrated communications campaign.

Make no mistake, getting Delahaye up and running was not easy. At the start, Katie also ran a public relations agency to get the cash necessary to build Delahaye. By late 1988 the agency folded. Katie concentrated on Delahaye.

The year 1991 was a turning point. I had met Katie the previous year. I knew instinctively that this was a smart, special person. She was so alive, so fresh with curiosity, drive, and boundless energy.

Even so, the day we met she was down. Her father had just died. Her car had broken down in a driving rainstorm, and she had been robbed. Other mishaps and broken relationships soon followed.

That day Katie wondered if it was really all worth it now that her father was gone. Maybe she would just sail around the world for a year, read some books, listen to some music—indulge her passions.

It doesn't so much matter what you do in particular,
so long as you have your life.
—HENRY JAMES

Each fall when I see Katie, I hear about the coming sailing trip. "I still get that itch," Katie admits. "I still really, definitely get that itch. I was just thinking, in fact, that I might like to sell the Delahaye Group, then go write books and run for a political office."

Such words are more a ritual among friends. Delahaye has hit its stride. After job-hopping for a dozen years, CEO Katie has found her happiness. She has been building and leading Delahaye as a unique, values-based employer and service provider.

And where is she doing it? Right back in New Hampshire, living in beautiful country in a rustic home. "What's that expression?" she asks me. "It's something like, 'You can journey to the ends of the earth in your search for success, but if you're lucky, you'll find your happiness in your own backyard.' I guess I've done that in a way, but it's been my way."

> **Success is getting what you want.**
> **Happiness is wanting what you get.**
> —WARREN BUFFETT

A $5 million company with a roster of Fortune 500 clients, Delahaye today services customers in forty countries and has newly established offices in Amsterdam, the Netherlands, and Montevideo, Uruguay.

Katie Paine saw Delahaye as her opportunity to create a democratic workplace—something she had never experienced. In her words, "I dreamed of creating a company where I'd like to work. It would have great bosses, challenging work, and everyone would have a voice in decision making. I wanted people to be able to find their true gifts, and I wanted the company to be able to employ those gifts. So for me, the family-friendly, consensus-driven management style was a no-brainer."

She spent the first five years trying to accomplish her goal, eventually learning that, in business, complete democracy can lead to total anarchy. She notes, "There are tough decisions that need to be made, and they need to be made in a timely fashion. Also, some things just have to get done. I didn't modify my ideals, but we had to rethink how we could carry it out."

Still, Katie was able to create an exciting workplace, both in the design of people's jobs and in the design of Delahaye itself. "We have a lot of flexibility here—people may work part-time or full-time, from home or the office—and have created a work environment in New Hampshire that everyone truly enjoys," Katie says with pride. "We have always requested that any wood used for building be responsibly harvested—pretty radical in a state where these words had probably never been uttered previously. In 1992 they laughed at us."

Katie exacted some of these same standards from suppliers. While she educated the office staff about pre- and post-consumer waste, she threatened the company's accounting firm with dismissal unless they changed the paper and covers of Delahaye's annual statements.

She also is known throughout the Northeast for her Ben & Jerry-style parties. Whether it's Bastille Day on July 14 or Boxing Day on December 26, Katie makes sure everyone—employees, friends, and local residents—is invited and has fun. That spirit carries through to the daily work: "We measure a company's perceived image," Katie points out. "The work can be tedious at times. So I do my best to see that the environment is exciting and uplifting."

> **Service is the very purpose of life.**
> **It is the rent we pay for living on the planet.**
> —Marian Wright Edelman

Responsibility to the community is in Katie's blood. "In my previous jobs, I didn't really have much of a chance to give back. At Delahaye, it is integral to who we are," Katie maintains. "Even our newsletters and Web site, though intended to attract business, are there to help educate people about our world and the important social issues we face."

From the early 1990s, when the company really could not afford to donate time or resources, Delahaye maintained a number of pro bono accounts. For example, it helped billionaire Alfred Taubman position his efforts to privatize the Michigan high schools. Any liberal just cause was a cause Delahaye would assist—even before the company was profitable.

"A lot of this stuff is easy," Katie confesses. "The tough choices in Delahaye's history came when sales slowed. At one point we were losing $50,000 a month. That was, of course, when a major tobacco company, a nuclear power company, and W. R. Grace all called us to bid on work for them. I turned them all down, but not without facing some pretty horrified looks from my sales department."

I ask people why they have deer heads on their walls.
They always say because it's such a beautiful animal.
There you go. I think my mother is attractive,
but I have photographs of her.
—ELLEN DEGENERES

Today Delahaye has partners around the world who think nothing of working for tobacco companies or nuclear power companies. "I have no control over them," says Katie. "But I find that when I explain to them that we are in the business of helping companies improve the effectiveness of their communications, and I elaborate on the social implications of that effectiveness for the companies under question, they come around to our point of view.

"I think the lesson," Katie states, "is that the balance between your social mission and your business reality is something that never goes away. Like Mark, I found that my involvement in SVN (Social Venture Network) helped me realize it was truly possible to incorporate into my business my social imperative to right social wrongs and leave the world a better place. That doesn't mean that there are not tough decisions to be made.

"Today, we need capital to continue our growth. And, as you know, capital comes with strings attached. The question I'm facing is, do I sell out and abandon control over our social mission, because with the money I could get I could do so much more, or do we continue on a path that may eventually mean we're too small to survive."

The best way out is always through.
—ROBERT FROST

Katie will find her way. She will do it as with everything else she has ever done. Try it, learn from the mistakes, try something else, learn from new mistakes, and so on—until it fits just right.

Currently unattached, Katie travels constantly. A highly sought-after teacher, corporate speaker, and writer on business, entrepreneurship, and media, Katie is known well beyond her New Hampshire borders.

"I didn't realize it before, but Delahaye is the vehicle through which I can change the world. It's my platform. It allows me to leverage our research, our brand of doing business, and our concerns for society to influence others in their businesses."

Update: On March 15, 1999, Medialink Worldwide acquired the Delahaye Group, Inc. Katie will be president of the Delahaye Medialink Division. As she wrote me: "It was essentially your call that made me see this deal was good for all concerned. I get real money for a change to enable me to have more of a life . . . and it's a means to see my immediate dreams and visions become a reality." Longer term, it will allow Katie to concentrate more time on her passion for politics and public service.

Katharine Delahaye Paine is always stretching herself a

little bit further, persistent in finding the place she truly fits. Del Paine must be awfully proud of his little girl.

> **If we don't change, we don't grow.**
> **If we don't grow, we aren't really living.**
> —GAIL SHEEHY

✳

Lifelines

The Greek philosopher Heraclitus observed that "no man ever steps in the same river twice, for it's not the same river and he's not the same man."

As we change and the world changes, finding a place in it is not easy. The target keeps moving, and we are works in progress. We carry with us societal and parental expectations about who we are and what is best for us to do. Parental love can be as blind as any other kind.

Few people know what they want to do at the start of their careers. Finding your calling, your dream, is usually a process of growth that requires trial and error. So ask yourself: What are the things I don't want to do in my job, my career, and, ultimately, my life? What kind of work am I doing when the time seems to fly? Or when it doesn't?

Your path is often one of eliminating what you don't like to do rather than trying to come up with what you do like.

Katie Paine's career included many "mistakes" that allowed her to take the steps that eventually led her to form her own company, a business in which she uses the skills developed in more than a dozen jobs. Following the trail of her fall career transitions points up how she tried to eliminate at least one part of the work she didn't like in her old job when she selected her next job.

Personal trial and error is inevitably painful, but suffering is optional. It is all part of the preparation for your life's work; as Abraham Lincoln said, "I will study and get ready, and perhaps my chance will come."

Katie was able to follow her path because she did not tie her identity too closely to any one job, and she continued to gather a range of experiences useful for the next.

Mistakes are the price we pay for a full life.
—Sophia Loren

PART 4

WHERE CAN YOU GO?

Free Your Spirit

CHAPTER 10

✳

LIVE A LIFE,
NOT A RÉSUMÉ

Nick Gleason's Livelihood

May you live all the days of your life.
—JONATHAN SWIFT

**You will become as small as your controlling desire;
as great as your dominant aspiration.**
—JAMES ALLEN

We all hope to live lives that mean something, lives that have a purpose, make a difference, leave a legacy. And we can all do that—no matter our background or socioeconomic station.

In 1996 I wrote an article called "Papa Nat and Mr. McMullen." It told the story of how two men from completely different backgrounds led lives of significance.

Papa Nat, as his family called him, held on to his textile mills in the Northeast long after it made economic sense to do so. The family lost most of its wealth when the mills finally went bankrupt in the 1970s, but thousands of third- and fourth-generation millworkers had jobs for ten to fifteen additional years. His story is told in the last chapter of the book.

Mr. McMullen grew up in Chelsea, one of Boston's poorest sections. He never finished primary school, and he made his living with his hands in a variety of steady, blue-collar construction jobs. Speaking in sometimes unintelligible broken English, this jubilant, Irish Catholic *mensch* communicated what was in his heart through his deeds.

John McMullen and his wife, Mary, had seven children. Times were tough, but they always found a way. Against the customs of the times, John helped with the housework and loved raising those children in between his frequent double shifts. All seven graduated high school, and most finished college as well. Today they are teachers, accountants, and middle managers.

John and Mary recognized that many children in Boston were not as fortunate as theirs. So in the 1990s, with their children grown, the McMullens took in over two hundred foster children, many with disabilities. Each one got plenty of love, warmth, and rules to grow on.

John expanded his homestead into a cheerful boarding-house with a few dozen bedrooms. Some of the children remain at the house to this day. And there's always a plate of hot spaghetti waiting for another kid who needs a home and a lot of love.

> **What we do is nothing but a drop in the ocean,**
> **but if we didn't do it, the ocean would be one drop less.**
> —MOTHER TERESA

What prevents many of us from making a difference? From being the people we want to be? From leading the life we want to live, a life of service and fulfillment? As Mark Twain perceptively observed: "Such tendency toward doing good as is in men's hearts would not be diminished by the removal of the delusion that good deeds are primarily for the sake of No. 2 instead of for the sake of No. 1."

When I ask my colleagues and friends what stops them, it is usually one of two things. The first is a feeling of powerlessness. What can I do about starvation in Africa? The homeless in America?

The simple answer is found in a young girl's words:

> Thousands of starfish had washed ashore.
> A little girl began throwing them
> In the water so they wouldn't die.
> "Don't bother, dear," her mother said.

"It won't make any difference."
The girl stopped for a moment,
Looked at the starfish in her hand.
"It will make a difference to this one."

The second obstacle involves two key forces in our culture. One is money, what I call the "M" thing. The other is what I call the "S" thing, the status thing.

The "S" thing is my shorthand for the external status and reputation attached to your name, your identity, your place in your world. It might come from where you work, what you do, or what you own. When you get caught up in it, both your expectations and, most especially, the expectations of others soar. A particular path, a particular way of behaving, is expected. What happens if it is not necessarily your way?

That's the dilemma I encountered as a young professor. When I glanced into the future one thoughtful night, I realized that building a résumé of positions and accomplishments, while nice to do, was not how I wanted to live my life.

I didn't much care about how my obituary might read in the newspapers. I was more interested in the *eulogy.* By that I mean that I was more interested in how I might touch people with my life.

Two comments came to mind. One was that of an eight-year-old boy who described what happens when you die: "Your body breaks up into thousands of pieces and goes into all the people whose lives you have touched. That way you live in them always."

That was the life I wanted to live. Or, as Dr. Martin Luther King Jr. put it so beautifully: "Every now and then I think about my own death, and I think about my own funeral. And if you get somebody to deliver the eulogy, tell them not to talk too long. Tell them not to mention that I have a Nobel Peace Prize. Tell them not to mention that I have three or four hundred other awards. I'd like for somebody to say that day that Martin Luther King Jr. tried to give his life serving others. I'd like for somebody to say that Martin Luther King Jr. tried to love somebody. . . . Say that I was a drum major for justice . . . for peace . . . for righteousness. I just want to leave a committed life behind."

> **I have walked the earth for thirty years and,**
> **out of gratitude, want to leave some souvenir.**
> —Vincent van Gogh

It may seem curious that this chapter about leading a life of significance, instead of only accomplishment, profiles the youngest person in the book, Nick Gleason. But once you learn who Nick is, I think you will understand why.

At thirty his résumé has elements of a Gen-X fast tracker:

- Stanford Bachelor of Arts; Harvard Master of Business Administration; United States Senate intern for Rhode Island Republican John Chafee; Rotary Club International Scholarship finalist; staffer for *MacNeil/Lehrer NewsHour* and *Foreign Policy* magazine; Coro Foundation Fellow (national leadership program); field experience with Habitat for Humanity.
- Passed Foreign Service examination to enter diplomatic corps; Firestone Award at Stanford (for top 10 percent of honors theses); Echoing Green Foundation Fellowship at Harvard (one of 15 nationally).

In addition, Nick speaks fluent Spanish, worked on radio as a disc jockey, reporter, newscaster, news editor, and producer for five years, and began his own marketing, finance, and strategy consulting business (Gleason Associates) in 1994, with clients ranging from the Internet's Motley Fool to the United States Department of Health and Human Services.

He even spent a summer in manufacturing, almost taking a full-time job as a plant manager after business school.

If that is all you know about Nick, you know something, but you do not know *why* he is. You also know little about the enthusiastic, persevering heart that drives him to mix his idealism with capitalistic pragmatism.

> **If you ask me what I have come to do in this world . . .**
> **I will reply: I'm here to live my life out loud.**
> —ÉMILE ZOLA

Nick Gleason lives to shatter misconceptions about class, race, and possibilities. He bristles at black-and-white characterizations or at simplifications of others or of himself. In other words, he hates preconceptions and quick fixes.

He resists, sometimes impetuously, categories and boxes devised by others. In some ways he has fought against such distinctions his whole life. That is what drives him to overcome obstacles on the "messy road to success" as he tries to make a difference in our urban neighborhoods.

While attending Harvard Business School, Nick worked as a community organizer in an urban neighborhood. There he developed a network and skill set that led to the creation in 1997 of CitySoft, a technology company that hires urban residents.

"What you see in the media," Nick begins, "is each end of the spectrum. At one end, you hear about urban residents who have made it. They went to Ivy League colleges and are superstars in corporate America. At the other extreme, the nightly news is full of the stories on those who have turned to crime and drugs. The truth is that the vast majority are between those two endpoints.

"Urban neighborhoods have many underutilized workers who have tremendous potential. Part of what is necessary to realize that potential is opportunity. That's what CitySoft offers.

"At CitySoft, we do not 'save' people. That's not the way we view ourselves. That's the old-school view. We are in a business [outsourced Internet-development work] that badly needs more programmers. We are finding them in the urban neighborhoods. We work with urban technical training centers to find potential employees and then provide a positive developmental work environment."

The cultural initiation of new employees reveals more about Nick and CitySoft. On arrival, each person receives a copy of two books: Stephen Covey's *The Seven Habits of Highly Effective People* and M. Scott Peck's spiritual masterpiece, *The Road Less Traveled*. Each also receives a toy tortoise.

"I completely relate to the story of the tortoise and the hare," Nick explains. "The tortoise is the underdog who wins against the odds through determination and perseverance. It's his attitude that we at CitySoft relate to deeply.

"We don't want to be a hare—fast out of the blocks but ephemeral, without the staying power to be the winner in the end. We want to be here for a long time," emphasizes Nick.

Whether because of his youth or his membership in a generation seeking to forge a new paradigm, Nick is out to shatter the "either/or" mentality of assumed trade-offs. He wants to demonstrate that a business can be highly profitable and still accomplish community objectives. It is the world of the "and."

**If he was to become himself, he must find a way
to assemble the parts of his dreams into one whole.
—GEORGE ELIOT**

Nick Gleason will be a star someday. He's got the drive, the enthusiasm, the smarts. He is building a life with a patchwork of experiences that defies simple categories. He has the courage to be and to do, not worrying about "how it looks." He has the strength to be unique, unlike many others with his academic and professional background.

Nick has been in the corridors of power and the conference rooms of policy makers. His résumé reflects that. But CitySoft owes much to Nick Gleason's less visible résumé.

Nick spent the summer before Stanford cleaning men's rooms at Rhode Island state beaches. After college he slept on couches and floors for months. He even experienced the humiliation of applying for food assistance.

In CitySoft's first year, the company's conference room was Nick's 1984 Subaru station wagon—two hundred thousand miles on the clock and climbing. His corridors of power were a borrowed two hundred square feet at an urban nonprofit organization. His power concerns ran to gigabytes, RAM, and urban residents, not the corporate promotions, stock options, and Washington connections that concerned many of his colleagues in Harvard's class of 1997.

Nick Gleason serves as a high-tech bridge between Boston's predominantly minority, low-tech Roxbury, Dorchester, and Mattapan neighborhoods and the promise and prosperity of high-tech corporate America. When he speaks of CitySoft and urban development, he uses words such as "opportunity," "resources," "entrepreneurship," and "business"—not "charity," "philanthropy," "bureaucracy," and "welfare."

Nick Gleason is a pragmatic entrepreneur who is making an investment in urban neighborhoods. His hours are long, his personal life minimal. But then again, he is living his life and trying to help build the lives of others. However, in case you missed it, it hasn't been easy.

**To be independent of public opinion is
the first formal condition of achieving anything great.**
—GEORG WILHELM HEGEL

Nothing could have been more antithetical to the Gleason family tradition than going to business school.

"We had no context for business of any kind—never mind graduate business school—in our family," says Nick. His parents were actually embarrassed by the prospect and half-jokingly told their friends, "Yes, Nick's at Harvard Business School, but he doesn't want to make money."

For generations Nick's relatives had pursued lives of achievement in academia and public affairs. Several became renowned professors or respected journalists. Many also served their communities and their country in times of crisis.

Nick's parents, in particular, were powerful influences on him. A professor of Russian history at Brown University, his outgoing father spent a summer in Mississippi, organizing efforts to help enforce civil rights legislation in the crucial early days of the movement. The elder Gleason also served as a policy analyst and director at Washington's Kennan Institute, a distinguished center of Russian studies.

Nick's nurturing mother also provided him with a model of community and social activism. She had been a teacher, a writer, an environmental official, and a community activist. Her father had worked in the New Deal under Roosevelt. He wrote speeches for Adlai Stevenson and later edited *Harper's* magazine.

While Nick had some interests similar to those of his relatives, he made the mistake of judging himself and his accomplishments solely in their terms. As a result, he put a lot of pressure on himself to be as successful as his relatives.

**We must resemble each other a little
in order to understand each other,
but we must be a little different to love each other.**
—PAUL GÉRALDY

Much as he respected all this East Coast heritage, Nick chose to break with family tradition early on, beginning with his decision to pass up Harvard College in favor of going to Stanford, three thousand miles from his Rhode Island home.

Nick's sophomore year at Stanford was intensely introspective and often depressing, a time of confronting more deeply his need to "figure out who I was." More important, Nick had to come to terms with his relationship with his parents.

"My choices weren't always theirs," reflects Nick. "It became important for me to learn how to communicate my frustrations and opinions without feeling guilty, indulging in my own anger, or hurting them. I also wanted to make it clear that I needed their support and love—that I had to do this so I could move ahead in our relationship and in my life."

As Mother Teresa taught, "If you judge people, you have no time to love them." Nick and his parents grew closer. What he learned from his family relationships helped him then, and it helps him today in business.

"I try to be careful not to invalidate, not to control the experiences or perceptions of others," he says. "At CitySoft, I can control our Web site work. I can't control other people's perceptions about community development or race issues. So much is behind those belief systems."

**The world will never starve for want of wonders,
but for want of wonder.**
—G. K. CHESTERTON

Nick finished his experience at Stanford with four months in Seville, Spain, learning about other cultures, and then five months in post-Pinochet Chile, writing his thesis. After seventeen years of right-wing dictatorship, Chile had been taken over by the Left. It was another revelation for Nick.

"In Chile, the press would standardize and simplify, but Chileans were dealing with complex human and historical issues."

Nick saw how a philanthropic, charitable approach "can be sloppy and undermine all the good it is trying to do." It wasn't about categories like Right and Left—categories he doesn't believe in. It was about the Chilean people and honoring their experiences, their needs.

"I felt I could be a bridge between subcultures, like the ones I saw in Chile," Nick explains, "facilitating answers to questions in the areas people can come together on, not what divides them."

> **Don't judge each day by the harvest you reap, but by the seeds you plant.**
> —ROBERT LOUIS STEVENSON

Upon returning to the United States, Nick spent the next five years in highly diverse situations, many of them confusing or painful, but all of value to him "in a society that is very categorical, very divided."

He worked in labor unions and nonprofit organizations, in government and private enterprise, for a large company and as an entrepreneur, for conservatives and for liberals.

"These experiences were a way of having my assumptions challenged and my knowledge sharpened," he says. The path was not exactly paved with gold.

The year after graduating from Stanford, Nick's 1992 tax return showed a gross income of $68.75. But he felt comfortable with little or no money, and it caused him "to be creative." It also brought him to some deeply meaningful experiences that were not on the résumés written for him by his family or anyone else.

Right out of college, Nick went to work for public television's *MacNeil/Lehrer NewsHour,* then for *Foreign Policy* magazine—jobs that were in harmony with his father's work at Washington's famed Kennan Institute. In both places, though, he felt "people were fighting over who gets to interpret the world to other people. I wanted to be more of a participant."

He decided to leave Washington to go to Oakland, California, and work for Habitat for Humanity.

From Utah he called home to tell his family that he was set on this experience and not coming back. His parents didn't cheer, but they didn't disapprove, either, once they heard Nick's reasons. His father's parting words were, "You are going to do the Lord's work."

What we are looking for is a way of
experiencing the world in which we are living
that will open to us the transcendental.
—JOSEPH CAMPBELL

Sleeping on mattresses acquired from the Salvation Army, moving from one place to another, Nick subsisted on what the service community likes to call "psychic income." The $250-a-month stipend he received wasn't enough.

"Habitat is an amazing organization," Nick says. "But I began to feel increasingly uncomfortable with its fear of creating organizational bureaucracy. For example, there we were all working terribly hard and unable to get health insurance. Had something happened, we would have been hard-pressed to pay for appropriate care. I was a little un-comfortable about that."

Nick was beginning to wonder if working for the bet-terment of the world really did—or should—require such a trade-off. His situation got so bad that he felt forced to subject himself to what he still remembers as a degrading experience.

"I applied for free food from a local social service agency. It was a mistake to apply, but I did because I was determined not to rely on my family and was frustrated that I wasn't being paid enough for basic survival. I didn't want to play with being poor, either. Though I regret the decision, it was a powerful experience."

Nick found the application process itself to be demoraliz-ing, even though his situation was far different from that of everyone else there. But the really disturbing part was get-ting the free food.

"The very act of being a supplicant—the object of charity and pity—was extraordinarily disempowering," recalls Nick. "I only did it twice, but it was humiliating and drained some of the life out of me."

> **Lives based on having are less free**
> **than lives based on doing or being.**
> —WILLIAM JAMES

Nick was doing odd jobs in software consulting when he re-ceived a prestigious Coro Foundation fellowship. Intended for future national leaders in public service, Coro gave Nick an internship in business and as a union organizer.

It was action-oriented work, but he found it frustrating that there were almost no businesspeople in urban develop-ment. Equally frustrating, labor negotiations invariably con-sisted of two unyielding sides posturing for their own constituents, Nick says. Their mutual refusal to recognize each other's needs made intelligent solutions almost impossible.

During the one-year fellowship, he learned about computer technology and formalized his consulting work in Internet development and community organizing, calling himself Gleason Associates. Being accountable as an entrepreneur and having the opportunity to set his own ground rules energized him. People loved his sheer hustle. And no one ever asked for a résumé. His résumé was his network. Soon he was making good money, too.

Nick had freed himself from the résumé written of, by, and for others. He was free of the past, of external pressures. He had worked his way to a platform without ideology or stereotypes. He was a bridge between people of different convictions, backgrounds, and futures.

But he still hadn't found his place. Now what? Law school? Public policy? Neither. Nick chose business school. He was again writing his own kind of résumé.

I feel like I am diagonally parked in a parallel universe.
—STEVEN WRIGHT

Nick Gleason went directly from working in a tough Oakland housing project to the shores of the Charles River and its elite Harvard Business School. It was quite a change of scenery.

"I arrived, met some students, and began talking about jobs. When they found out that I did not know what McKinsey and Company or the Goldman Sachs Group were, they thought I must be from the moon."

In the world of top business schools, over 60 percent of graduates enter either management consulting or investment banking. McKinsey and Goldman are, respectively, the perceived pinnacles of these two industries. Nick Gleason was a fish out of water.

He found his own group at the school. It was a group of one. Often he was the only person in the class who even vaguely tried to express the views of organized labor, views that drew hisses and boos from his classmates.

Nick felt that the learning environment at Harvard, while teaching him much about business and decision making, created an atmosphere in which "students were petrified to say something different. And I was the pretty nice guy who just didn't get it, who was too often on the wrong side."

At home neither in the business world nor in the anti-business world, Nick wasn't so much a displaced person as someone still finding his place. It was a role he was getting used to.

As he admits: "I'm the kind of person who likes to go to nonprofits and talk about business, and go to Harvard Business School and talk about social issues. It's fun being called a conservative in one place and a Commie in another."

Nick learned, however, that "you don't get anything accomplished if you marginalize yourself. You still need to be you, but you need to find ways to talk with people you don't agree with. I began to remember all those little experiences I had and how to stick it out to make things happen," he says.

How can you be a Marxist and still have a Jacuzzi?
—LINDA KANE

Most unusual, Nick organized community projects throughout the week at the Dudley Street Neighborhood Initiative in the middle of Roxbury, the most *inner* of Boston's urban neighborhoods, rife with poverty and problems. This was the kind of extracurricular activity that is unheard of because of its nature and the heavy first-year workload at Harvard.

But service was in Nick's blood and the source of his sanity. "Getting other people energized gets me energized," he states. (He continues to exhibit incredible stamina today at CitySoft, often working eighteen to twenty hours a day, seven days a week.)

He spent the summer between his first and second years at business school working in a manufacturing plant, which nourished his interest in management-labor issues. If not for CitySoft, he says, he would have become a plant manager after graduation.

So why did Nick turn down a real job with a real salary in favor of the insecurity of being a novice entrepreneur? The choice he made wasn't easy. He needed permission to summon the strength, and he got it from some unexpected allies.

The first was Kate Snow, who combined a degree in education and a background in high technology to run a nearby social service organization, the Somerville Community Computing Center.

When Nick told Kate that he had contracts to build Web sites and was looking for someone to do them, Kate replied: "Great. We've got these urban kids found and trained by the MIT [Massachusetts Institute of Technology] Talent Search program. I'm looking for work to give them."

So Nick brought urban kids being trained in high tech together with customers looking for affordable Web sites. And it was through this project that he met his CitySoft cofounder, Jim Picariello.

Nick and Jim realized they had not one, but two businesses: there was the training and the Web-site development. But the venture wasn't profitable using the kids. The gap between the level of training needed and the skills demanded by the jobs was great.

After locating three training centers beyond MIT—the Urban League, Tent City, and the Mandela Housing Project— they decided to focus on Web site development and to hire older urban residents who were already trained. (In mid-

1999, Nick launched CitySkills, which provides resources over the Internet to help urban training organizations develop Internet-trained adults.)

Teachers open the door, but you must enter by yourself.
—ANCIENT CHINESE PROVERB

In that fall semester of his second year at Harvard, Nick took a class called "Managing Product Development." A popular, project-based course, it gave students a chance to start up a new product or even a new organization—on paper, anyway.

When Nick met with the course professor, Marco Iansiti, he hesitantly proposed the project he was already working on: "Web-site development with kids from urban neighborhoods." He explained his rationale to Marco: the untapped urban potential, the motivation of entrepreneurship and its impact on urban development, and the need for job development.

Marco's reply stunned Nick: "You've got to do this."

Enthused, Nick looked around for project partners. He found not one classmate who was interested. They were doing projects offered by Microsoft, Intel, and other industry heavyweights. Nick went it alone, forewarned by the words of John Stuart Mill: "Every great movement must experience three stages: ridicule, discussion, adoption."

By spring 1997 Nick and Jim were seriously considering the start-up. But the need for additional external validation remained. The opportunity costs for Nick were high, and even though he had developed a tolerance for risk, this was way out there. That was when Nick and I met. He says I helped.

We both were involved in Students for Responsible Business. That March we sat on a campus bench and talked for an hour. Before leaving, I told Nick that I had discussed what he was going to do with acquaintances at *The Wall Street Journal.*

Nick went away seething over my preannouncement. When he got home, ready to call and give me an earful, he found a message on his answering machine.

A couple of months later, when the bell sounded marking the end of the last business school exam, and with three weeks remaining until June graduation, Nick and Jim were already off and running with CitySoft.

The moment that one definitely commits one's self, then Providence moves, too.
—JOHANN WOLFGANG VON GOETHE

I like to call Nick "Harvard's hope." I believe he exemplifies the best of Harvard Business School. In his first year out, the school wrote two cases about him and featured him prominently in alumni magazines, next to Ira Jackson in one piece.

Nick does not like the moniker. While he concedes that Harvard is part of him and that its networks continue to help in a variety of ways, he sees the actual process of getting to CitySoft as separate from Harvard.

"I spent a lot of time writing down the things I cared about, my interests, and the best parts of past jobs," he explains. "I then tried to think of how I could capture as much as possible in one job. It's called CitySoft."

One year after he left Harvard Business School, Nick's CitySoft was exceeding expectations: revenue in the six figures and a small profit; a growing client list that included BankBoston Corporation, Polaroid Corporation, ITT Sheraton Corporation, and Siemens AG; and calls from the White House.

In its second year more management was brought in to

help with plans to set up operations in New York, San Francisco, Chicago, and Baltimore—although Nick continues to be careful in handling their expansion. So far he has focused on just one new office, in New York. Jack Smith, an NYU-trained lawyer, entrepreneur, and community activist, joined CitySoft in mid-1999 and began drawing from all of the Big Apple's urban communities to create a diverse team of Latinos, African-Americans, and Hassidim.

There is a lot at stake. The days of not being able to find a team for CitySoft at Harvard are long past. There is a team in place now. "We're in the deep end of the pool," says Nick. "We don't know how to swim. We had better learn quickly."

Profit *and* morality are a hard combination to beat.
—HUBERT HUMPHREY

The company has faced a media onslaught. Careful not to let expectations and promises exceed CitySoft's capabilities, Nick has nevertheless seen his urban programmers on CNN and CNBC, and articles have appeared in several newspapers and magazines.

Less than eight months after they began, Nick and Jim were featured in a substantial article on the front page of *The Wall Street Journal*'s second section (the result of that phone message on Nick's answering machine). In the résumé sweepstakes, Nick achieved a credential much admired by Harvard Business School graduates: the first member of the class of 1997 to have his picture (an artistic rendering) appear in the mighty *Journal*.

When scores of classmates e-mailed their congratulations, Nick could not help gloating a bit at the fact that accolades came from people who once refused to take him seriously—or could not relate to him at all.

The school asked him to speak to different groups of students and alumni four times that first year.

**I set as the goal the maximum capacity
that people have—I settle for no less. I make myself
a relentless architect of the possibilities of human beings.**
—BENJAMIN ZANDER

Nick Gleason has set out to build a world-class business. He isn't playing. He has no fallback. As he says, "It isn't like I've made $20 million and am now doing this as my reward. It's for real."

Without an escape hatch, there can be no way to hedge your bets. There can be no second chances either. For the people of CitySoft, that means total interdependence. "Everybody pretty much understands that their survival is tied to each other," says Nick.

Consider this e-mail from Nick to his colleagues after the company had some serious quality-control problems with a client. "We have worked long and hard to get to this point," he wrote. "We have a chance to make it as a company. We have a chance to make it for ourselves. We also have a chance to make a difference in urban neighborhoods all around the country.

"If we succeed, we break down misperceptions and stereotypes. If we fail, we confirm ignorance and bias.

"We are not the same people we were yesterday—by fate or luck, we have more opportunity and more responsibility than our peers—and for a while we need to rise to that challenge and give up whatever old beliefs prevent us from being the best in this business. It is all up to us; it is all in our hands."

**Many people have the wrong idea of what constitutes
true happiness. It is not attained through self-gratification,
but through fidelity to a worthy purpose.**
—HELEN KELLER

If you think of the creation of CitySoft as another credit on the résumé, you're wrong. For Nick it's all about high expectations, about standards.

"I'm not ideological," he professes. "I'm interested in what works, what is self-sustaining. We don't want to be subject to other people's ways of doing things."

If CitySoft can't do "what we need to do to be of value in the marketplace, it's over," Nick says bluntly. "If the people of CitySoft can't do what they need to do to be of value in the marketplace, then guess what? I'm in trouble, because I respect them and I'm depending on them. We all understand that our livelihood, our success, depends on one another.

"I'm not buffering anyone from reality. This business is all about high performance and high standards. It has to be."

Anyone who proposes to do good must not expect people to roll stones out of his way, but must accept his lot calmly, even if they roll a few more upon it.
—ALBERT SCHWEITZER

Nick has not taken a breather since day one, but he does take time to reflect on what is happening: "I've been able to take an activist approach to learning because I'm not crippled by failure. As long as I'm learning and growing, more opportunities will come. I just hang in there and know it will happen.

"At first, CitySoft was terrifying. Now, it's getting to be fun. I'm stretched. And the right people have stuck by me, even after we made mistakes. A handful of people have taken me under their wing. My greatest asset today is my network of friends.

"I think about what I'm doing, what I like and don't like. It can be painful, but you must find things that are a good fit with your personality. You're going to make a lot of mistakes on the way. Starting a business is a messy and chaotic process."

In 1999 CitySoft moved to the Kendall Square area, partially because their former space was no longer available, partially as a result of their growing need for space.

Nick explains: "The biggest surprise for me has been the experience of 'success.' I have always felt like the underdog and was envious of all these successful people. I thought they had it so easy and were just gliding along.

"I know better now. I found that I could achieve things through hard work and compensate for my self-perceived lack of talents through determination. The lesson for me was that happiness and satisfaction is more about effort and character than it is about pedigree and book smarts. That's why I relate so closely to the tortoise.

"While I never feel successful, we have had our share of excitement. Still, success doesn't look or feel anything like I thought. It's a process of handling lots of failures as just bumps along the road.

"We want to legitimize that a talented technology labor force is available in urban areas and catalyze other companies to hire here, too. When you have a mission like that, the bumps are so much easier to handle. And I love being an entrepreneur. If CitySoft isn't it, it's close."

Victor Hugo wrote, "An invasion of armies can be resisted, but not an idea whose time has come." For social entrepreneur Nick Gleason, the armies are coming, too—armies of young, committed, talented men and women who, like himself, want to live a life of significance. It's a life too big to fit into any one résumé.

I just thought it was an honor to serve.
—JOHN GLENN

*

Lifelines

Among Warren Buffett's pearls of wisdom is this one: "I always worry about people who say, 'I'm going to do this for ten years; I really don't like it very well. And then I'll do this. . . .' That's a little like saving up sex for your old age."

Buffett doesn't believe much in résumé building or taking jobs just for the money. He believes in doing work you enjoy—work that contributes to your own well-being and serves others.

The key question is simply stated by Gail Sheehy: "What are you prepared to give up in your material life to try to make your dream come true?" Put another way, what résumé-building, brand-name experience are you willing to forgo to make that dream come true? And if not now, what are you waiting for?

Ultimately life is about making a difference. Experiencing work in diverse circumstances allows you to challenge assumptions about how things operate and about what's possible for you to accomplish. And while you may not be on the proverbial fast track, you are living a life of meaningful experiences—and that has a track of its own.

Nick never thought about how to plan out his life to get somewhere. Not that he never plans; rather, he doesn't *only* plan. Not that he doesn't reflect (he clearly thinks about what he has learned from each experience); rather, he does *more* than just reflect.

What Nick Gleason does is live a life of meaning, a life of significance.

Making a Life, Making a Living

This is the true joy in life:
The being used for a purpose
recognized by yourself as a mighty one.
The being a force of nature. . . .
—George Bernard Shaw

CHAPTER 11

✳

DON'T LET SUCCESS STAND IN THE WAY OF OPPORTUNITY

Alan Webber's Integrity

There is no security in life, only opportunity.

—MARK TWAIN

Two roads diverged in a wood, and I—
I took the one less traveled by,
And that has made all the difference.
—ROBERT FROST

There is an age-old tale about a man who goes for a walk in a forest previously unexplored by any other human. He gets lost and wanders for hours, trying to find his way out. He tries many paths, but with no success.

When he comes upon another person, he cries out, "Thank God for another human being. Can you show me the way out?" The man replies, "No, I am lost, too."

The first man is dismayed, but the second one says, "Don't worry. We can tell each other which paths we've already tried without success. That will help us find our way out."

To venture causes anxiety.
Not to venture is to lose oneself.
—SÖREN KIERKEGAARD

I love risk takers and risk taking. I love the mystery, the unpredictability, the not knowing. I particularly like successful people who don't let their success stand in the way of life's next opportunity. After all, serendipity is often just around the corner.

"What's the worst that could happen?" I reply each time I am asked about taking a "career risk," about "going for it."

228

"But what if it doesn't work out?" the questioner invariably counters.

I often answer by talking about love: Where else do we see people taking bigger risks than for the hope of love?

Over the years I have learned that it isn't *what* you have in your life that counts, but *whom* you have in your life. I learned about risks—calculated risks taken with integrity and honesty—from a friend who became an accountant.

An accountant who takes risks? Neither this accountant nor unassuming, often self-deprecating Alan Webber, the subject of this chapter, is the type of person you would expect to be a risk taker. They are just two people doing what they need to do to be who they want to be. To have fun. To live the life they want to live. That requires risk taking.

The accountant is Pablo Lancella. Pablo and I met in prep school, and he remains one of my closest friends. Pablo taught me about taking risks through the sport of wrestling, a sport in which I could never reach my potential because I feared losing—that is, until Pablo helped me find my way out of the forest in 1968.

Pablo is a first-wave Cuban American, a member of one of the well-to-do families that fled Cuba when Castro came to power, leaving everything behind to start anew in Miami, Florida.

Pablo and I were two of the three scholarship students in our prep school class. We played all three of our sports together. The high point of *my* athletic experience was watching Pablo win a wrestling match.

The New England Prep School championships were held at our school the year we were juniors. We had a very good team, winning all of our matches and even our scrimmages against the best high school teams, none of which scored a point on us.

I had a terrible tournament—a second seed who was knocked out early. Pablo was seeded second, too, having lost badly earlier in the year to three-time champion Compton

Chase. We all knew Chase was unbeatable. He had not lost a match in league or national tournaments in four years.

You miss 100 percent of the shots you never take.
—WAYNE GRETZKY

I know all about "going for it" in sports. Invariably the champions are those who go for it on the big points. But wrestling is different from most other sports. You have to confront yourself as much as any opponent. Wrestling is so personal, so tied up in a young man's image of self.

In front of the hometown crowd, Pablo went for it in the finals. He played to his strength—takedowns—by letting Chase up, giving him free points, then taking him down again.

It was a risky strategy, for as good as Pablo was, tall, lanky Chase was considered one of the best ever at takedowns. But short, muscular Pablo tried something new: he stayed down on one knee instead of standing up completely, so as not to give Chase a chance to grab his legs. (The one time Pablo forgot and stood up for a moment, Chase took him down instantly.)

The strategy was a complete surprise. No one ever tried to match Compton Chase in takedowns—that is, until Pablo Lancella tried it.

And Pablo won. Yes, he did. I can still see his face as he came off the mat—stunned, elated, tears streaming down his cheeks. He was even named outstanding New England wrestler over a heavy favorite in another weight class who was a national champion.

The biggest surprise for me, however, was my own euphoria. I was not normally happy for a friend when I myself had messed up. I was usually jealous. This was especially

230

true in competitive sports, which is such a large part of our identity at that age.

But what Pablo did that day was, in my eyes, so extraordinary, so complete, that I still get chills when I visualize the match. He went for it and succeeded. I could not have been more excited if it had happened to me, because in a way it had.

Today Pablo has created a life that blends his continued love for sport with the living he makes as the head of his own small accounting company. It took some career risks mixed with a little patience to integrate the two. But he finally did it without any real risk. After all, he was just being Pablo, the wrestler.

Fortune favors the audacious.
—DESIDERIUS ERASMUS

In the 1980s I regularly surveyed the second-year MBA students who were taking my retailing course. Each year well over 90 percent said they were taking the course to learn how to make more money, plain and simple.

In the 1990s I have introduced other students to the concept of making a life while making a living. I begin my seminars by recounting the results of that twenty-year study of 1,500 business graduates described earlier, in chapter 1. (If you recall, 40 percent of those who "risked" their financial futures by doing what they loved became millionaires, while less than 1 percent who focused on money made millions.)

After pondering the findings, my students invariably ask: "What happened to the other 60 percent of the 'risk takers' who pursued what they loved? Did they go down the tubes?" None ask about the other 99 percent who pursued money.

It took me a while to understand the question.

All adventures, especially into new territories, are scary.
—SALLY RIDE

At top ten business schools, I realize, we nurture conservative behavior. Our students work hard to find clear answers and sure things. If anything, they learn to avoid undue risk. Many also wind up fearing the unknown. Some are paralyzed by it. We have forgotten the words of Yeats: "Education is not filling a bucket but lighting a fire."

I learned from visits to other schools.

At Babson Business School, MBAs questioned the measurement system: "You're talking about taking chances to find purposeful work. Why use a financial benchmark to measure success?" At Simmons Business School, an audience of vibrant women students pushed me into clarifying my whole thesis: The biggest risk—the one you must avoid—is failing to pursue your passion, the thing you feel you were born to do.

"Do what you love," I told the students. "Whether or not money follows is not vital. What is vital is that you won't be wasting your life. You won't be as likely to say later, 'I wish I had,' or ask, 'What if . . . ?'"

As retired International Business Machines Corporation executive Richard Imershein told them: "I advise you to dream. I believe one must have a dream, and it must be refreshed regularly or you lose it. It is that dream of youth that you shouldn't lose, for it is only then that you know it can be done.

"As we age," Imershein continued, "we keep being told that it can't be done, and we listen and lose our dreams. What might you risk to get there? Probably a lot less than you risk not getting there."

Just ask Alan Webber.

232

**Throw your heart over the fence
and the rest will follow.**
—NORMAN VINCENT PEALE

"The things I find essential to my world are authenticity, honesty, being true to yourself, caring about something you believe is larger than yourself, working with people who share that belief, loving what you're doing, and trusting in something you don't understand."

Those words were spoken by Alan Webber. You may know him as a founding editor of *Fast Company,* my favorite business magazine, but that's only what he is.

For who he is and where he's going, reread the eloquent words above.

Alan has achieved impressive things by taking chances in his career while always remaining faithful to who he is. Today he crusades for workplaces that combine significance and pleasure. "If it isn't fun, don't do it," is an oft heard Webber mantra around the office. He just can't imagine anyone working any other way.

His monthly magazine provides tools that can improve your business, but they may be even more potent for changing your life. Better still, they can bring your business and your life into alignment.

Getting there certainly wasn't easy for Alan, especially in the risky magazine publishing industry—and particularly so because he had given up success as well as security at a prestigious job to do it.

Alan recalls, "I went from being visible and validated to having the door slammed shut behind me. The phone calls stopped, the speaking offers dried up . . . the screen went blank. But it gave me just the chance I needed to make a whole new bunch of friends and to build a life and a living I couldn't have imagined at the time."

And that's just what Alan Webber did.

**The real social revolution is the switch from a life
largely organized for us . . . to a world in which
we are all forced to be in charge of our own destiny.**
—Charles Handy

A 1998 cover story in *Fast Company* described the advent of what writer Daniel Pink called America's "free agent nation." The story talked about the twenty-five million people, or 16 percent of the labor force, "who have swapped the false promise of security for the personal pledge of authenticity" as self-employed, independent contractors or as temps.

Not surprisingly, "authenticity" is also good for your personal health. According to a Johns Hopkins study, researchers found that those with little autonomy in their work are 70 percent more likely to die from heart disease than are employees who have high levels of control over their work.

The 84 percent of U.S. workers who are not free agents are experiencing career upheavals, too, as employment contracts vanish. The bravest seize change as an opportunity rather than suffer it as a disaster.

In the final analysis, don't we all become part of the "free agent nation"? Free agency raises the primal question Why work? It forces you to think about what you want to do with your life. The answer, in Alan's own words, is "to achieve beautiful synchronicity between who you are and what you do, assume your own shape rather than fit into some corporate box."

**There is a growing legion of businesspeople
who are hungry to build something of enduring character
on a set of values they can be proud of.**
—Jim Collins

"The journey," Alan says, "is not really about integration or balance, but about fun and feeling that you are serving a larger purpose—that you and your team were born to succeed at that purpose. Just make sure you don't do anything you don't want to do.

"And make sure you tell the truth—your truth. Say what you know, even to your boss. It's how you are of value to the company and how you feel great about what you do."

Alan Webber never had a grand plan. From the beginning he simply pursued a range of interests so wide as to border on restlessness. And at each step of his career, he took risks and plunged into unknown territory. The unknown just happened to be the place he could flourish best.

It hasn't been pure, unmitigated success. There were times when he hung on just from a sense of duty, times when he felt inadequate. But he always told his truth and was honest about his failings. Not one morning in his life did Alan Webber need to turn his face away from the image in the mirror. This unflinching attitude kept opening new opportunities, more chances to succeed.

"When you put yourself in what you feel is the right place for you—for who you are, who you are trying to be—and you do it with integrity and honesty, things happen. Luck happens. You end up on your feet. Just keep your eyes and heart open," Alan advises, "and have a little patience."

**In the great scheme of things, what matters
is not how long you live, but why you live,
what you stand for and are willing to die for.**
—Paul Watson

Alan's father had patience, but misfortune changed his path. Joe Webber was on the way to earning a master's degree in history at the University of Missouri when his father died, obliging Joe to leave school to support the family.

After serving in World War II and trying a host of jobs, Joe became a sales manager at Stanley Photo. Unable to teach history, he collected history books and made do by volunteering for the Missouri State Historical Society.

One could say that Joe's life was unfulfilled. Events forced him to work—albeit successfully—at a business career instead of the calling he heard from the tomes of history. But if you think that, you read the wrong book on Joe Webber's life.

Joe found another way. Indirectly he spent his time at what he loved, his history books. And as his years accumulated, he built quite a library of friends who loved those books as much as he did. The capstone of his passionate preoccupation was eventually becoming the historical society's hardworking president.

Joe and his wife, Joey (Josephine), became only Joey in 1996. The family was proud to give Joe's collection to the historical society. That was not the essence of his legacy for sons Alan and Mark.

"Dad touched so many lives," Alan recalls. "After he died, I ran into people who would tell me things like 'Your father was the sweetest guy. We all loved him here on the West Coast. Each time he would come, he'd bring us all peaches from the Midwest.' This is the kind of stuff you take with you."

I must Create a System or be enslav'd by another Man's.
—WILLIAM BLAKE

Alan Webber set out to live a different story. At St. Louis Country Day School, he was the editor of the school paper, played sports year-round, and was considered a student leader. He also began his career as the "designated bullshit disturber"—what I like to call a "DBD."

"Telling the truth for me was all about trying to make a difference by being honest about what I saw. And what I saw was the need for racial integration. So I wrote regular editorials on integration, much to the administration's dismay."

At Amherst College Alan majored in English and continued to "do everything," which included playing football and editing the college newspaper. His editorials were on the need for coeducation.

Upon graduation in 1971, Alan headed for Portland, Oregon, what he calls a "high-quality place to live." He became a dishwasher in a French restaurant, helped start the *Oregon Times* newspaper, and then left the country to go trekking in the Carpathian Alps in Romania.

He returned to Portland, where his work at the *Oregon Times* led to a chance encounter with a young city councilman, Neil Goldschmidt, who was running for mayor. Goldschmidt won, and Alan found himself writing speeches and serving as a policy adviser to one of the country's most exciting young urban leaders.

As Alan recalls, "It was fun. I didn't need much money and was doing work that mattered to me: helping develop a population strategy by which the city hoped to hold on to middle-class families with children, the kind of people who, in other parts of the country, were fleeing the cities for the suburbs."

It was important work. Alan didn't want to scc Portland become "another L.A., with only the rich and the poor." It was also how he met Frances Diemoz, a professional architect and planner, who was evaluating the impact of the freeway on the city. "She was killing freeways surreptitiously," Alan chides, "I was doing it overtly." The professional had met the politician.

When President Jimmy Carter appointed Neil Goldschmidt secretary of transportation, Alan and Frances, now married, went to Washington. Alan continued as Neil's "policy and speech guy." Neil liked Alan's willingness to speak honestly, even when the news was not good. "You are not going to make a contribution if you don't say what you think," notes Alan, ever the DBD.

> **Never doubt that a small group of thoughtful,**
> **committed citizens can change the world.**
> **Indeed it is the only thing that ever has.**
> —MARGARET MEAD

Neil assigned Alan to keep track of the auto industry, arguably the critical industry in the late 1970s. The Japanese were taking over America's pride and joy, making Neil Goldschmidt's cabinet position highly visible.

"Globalization" was the new watchword, and immersion in global competition was work that engaged Alan at the deepest levels. It was work that mattered. The assignment ended abruptly when Ronald Reagan was elected president in 1980.

What next? Stay in Washington? Alan didn't want to be a political operative. So back to Portland he went. He loved the lifestyle, but what would he do? Journalism wasn't really appealing, either. When asked about Wall Street, he replied that he had no interest.

Rather, for Alan, "following the thread of what had gotten me turned on in Washington seemed to be a reasonably interesting next step."

> **The people who get on in this world are the people**
> **who get up and look for the circumstances they want,**
> **and, if they can't find them, make them.**
> —GEORGE BERNARD SHAW

When the Harvard Business School suggested that Alan expand on his auto industry work by writing a book about industrial competition, he decided to take a chance. Alan, Frances, four-year-old Adam, and newborn Amanda packed up for Boston, ostensibly for a year or two.

"It wasn't as though this were a career goal," says Alan. "It wasn't as if I had always wanted to be at the Harvard Business School. I was just following my gut and figured it would be work I could do well and that would lead somewhere.

"The auto industry was crashing. This was a hot issue. And the people at Harvard were clearly bright people. They didn't offer me a lot of money, but we didn't need a lot of money."

The book took three years. The impact of a historic, myth-shattering article, "Managing Our Way to Economic Decline," by Harvard faculty members Robert Hayes and Bill Abernathy, was felt throughout corporate America.

Hayes and Abernathy argued that the Japanese were beating us at our own game, not because of preferential political and financial treatment, but because they were superior managers. What industry could better be used to document this assertion than Alan's specialty, automobiles?

Alan was in the right place at the right time with the right credentials. The business school administration suggested that he come to work at the prestigious *Harvard Business Review.*

This wasn't even following a passion; it was more like throwing the dice. "I thought I'd go, take a chance, and see what working on a magazine was about," Alan says. "If it didn't work, I could always go look for other things to do."

In fact, it didn't work for Alan. Not at first, anyway. "The place was running on automatic pilot," he remembers. "The work experience was such that if you were in the doorway at five o'clock, you'd be run over by people leaving.

"I decided to stay for a year—I felt that as an obligation—and then I began to look around for other options."

**The odds against there being a bomb on a plane
are a million to one, and against two bombs
a million times a million to one.
Next time you fly, cut the odds and take a bomb.**
—BENNY HILL

In the fall of 1985 Professor Ted Levitt became the faculty editor at the *Harvard Business Review.* One of the most influential and creative marketing minds in the world, Levitt proceeded to turn *HBR* upside down.

Doing things differently, even at the venerable *Harvard Business Review,* is the only way Ted knows how to operate. He plays tennis the same way. He will try ten outrageous shots, and nine will fail, but the other will be so brilliant, you feel you should concede the match.

"He opened all the doors and windows," says Alan with a wide smile. The breezes brought in fresh air and new people, but they also blew out others, not always benignly.

When Ted brought Alan in for a talk, he asked him what he wanted. To his own surprise, Alan found himself demanding, "Either I get to run this place, or I'm out of here."

"It was not a planned conversation," Alan says, "but it was the right thing to say. If in a moment of stark honesty you looked at my situation, those were the only sensible options.

"Hey, the more you put up with, the more you're going to get. To work for somebody else at that point would have been stupid. I was dissatisfied, and nobody else was going to fix that. Besides, when you're up against it, the truth has a way of blurting itself out."

Alan had taken a big risk. To his surprise, Ted took him on. Request accepted. "Show me what you can do," Ted bellowed. Now what? Be careful what you ask for; you just might get it, was Alan's first thought.

He would have to perform. In a few months this DBD would become the managing editor.

**Everything is the result of change . . . there is nothing
Nature loves so well as to change existing forms
and to make new ones like them.**
—MARCUS AURELIUS

Thus began a very exciting time, not just for Alan, but for
the *HBR*. Ted welcomed Alan's public policy background,
and Alan made the most of it. He began by bringing in new
voices with fresh, unconventional approaches to business—voices not usually heard in the pages of the staid
HBR. The voices came first from a Communist and later
from a movie actor.

After an article based on a transcript of a speech by Soviet
leader Mikhail Gorbachev, Alan began his "Statesman as
CEO" series in the July/August 1986 *HBR*. That issue featured
an interview with Helmut Schmidt, the former chancellor of
West Germany. Two issues later he was given credit as managing editor, serving under faculty editor Professor Ted
Levitt.

Through March 1990 Alan was in "Candyland." The musty,
workmanlike style of the old publication was giving way to
something that was thought-provoking and engaging. Both
the appearance and tone of the magazine were revamped.

The changes to the conservative, sixty-year-old publication were controversial, to say the least. "What are those car-
toons doing in *HBR?* It's not supposed to be *The New
Yorker!*" was heard in the hallways of the business school.

People were talking about the *Harvard Business Review.*
People were reading the *Harvard Business Review*—and
looking forward to reading it again.

Ted loved it. So did Alan.

Subscriptions skyrocketed. The entire staff was jubilant.
The attitude was, "Following the rules will not get the job
done. Getting the job done is no excuse for following the
rules," jokes Alan.

**He broke fresh ground—because he had the courage
to go ahead without asking whether others
were following or even understood.**
—DAG HAMMARSKJÖLD

Alan commissioned a bylined piece from Robert Redford about environmental negotiation. Entitled "Searching for Common Ground," it offered fresh arguments in support of a new business paradigm. Tackling another previously unexplored topic, the *HBR* also ran a Felice Schwartz article that famously defined the professional woman's "mommy track" predicament. Basketball coach Red Auerbach wrote about building a great team.

It wasn't just readers who noticed. The revamped *HBR* was twice nominated for a National Magazine Award. *The New York Times* covered the story of its resurgence. *HBR* stories were being picked up throughout the national media, stirring debate.

And a new breed of staff member populated the office, "a group of people who were having a blast," as Alan describes them. "That is happiness; to be dissolved into something complete and great," wrote Willa Cather.

For Alan this was exciting, important work. He was making a difference at a periodical that was making a difference to its readers. Backed by all the prestige and resources of a great university, the new *Harvard Business Review* was redefining the discussion of business and questioning what business should and would be in the future.

The euphoria lasted four years. Spring 1990 brought several changes in management. For Alan and the *HBR,* a rough patch ensued.

Some changes were symptomatic of the magazine publishing business in general; some were particular to *HBR,* a magazine that also maintains a relationship to a business school. Other changes arose from the difficulties of mixing a new group with the old guard.

Alan stuck it out for two more years. He felt he owed that much to the people he had hired, and he didn't want to give up too easily on something that had been such a great experience, something in which he had invested so much.

But, in the end, he sensed his own failure. He felt he had made too many accommodations, publishing articles he didn't believe in, giving in and going along when he really didn't want to. He had taken a chance and stayed on, and the risk had gone bad. It wasn't fun, and Alan wasn't telling his truth anymore.

At the same time, he thought: If this isn't fun anymore, why don't we do our own magazine? "We" meant Alan and Bill Taylor, another former *HBR* editor who had already left to write a book. "So, we started talking about it," Alan says.

They talked for six months, asking and answering a lot of questions, clipping articles they liked, collecting magazines they liked, gathering direct mail packages that impressed them.

> **The Graceful Exit . . . means leaving what's over without denying its validity or its past importance in our lives. It involves a sense of future, a belief that every exit line is an entry, that we are moving on, rather than out.**
> —ELLEN GOODMAN

Alan felt like a fraud at the office. No longer committed emotionally, he still tried to give it his best. His integrity insisted on that. But how honest was he being with himself, with the staff?

One day, "the switch got thrown," he recalls. "I could no longer in good conscience recruit people to work at *HBR* because I knew I wasn't going to be there. And they could sense it, too."

Expediency says stay till you find something else. Use the office space and the phones—and especially the cachet that goes with a place like the *Harvard Business Review*. Everyone and anyone you want will return your calls. Expediency says leave when you find the right thing.

Integrity says get out.

Alan Webber was forty-two years old, with a wife and two children. His job at the *HBR* wasn't only a high-paying position, it was prestigious. It opened many doors. Now he was talking about chucking all this success for the great unknown—a very dangerous unknown to boot: the magazine business is notorious for devouring its young. The publishing world is littered with the corpses of start-up magazines that didn't make it.

Fortunately for Alan, his wife, Frances, made it easier. The daughter of a maverick, she was more of a risk taker, and she wasn't particularly fond of Alan's colleagues anyway. But ten-year-old Amanda felt "a disturbance in the force." She worried about money and sensed that her father was about to do something "risky."

As for Alan himself, he wasn't scared. His was the bliss of ignorance. "I didn't know what I was getting into, so how could I be scared?

"Human beings are propelled forward in ignorance," he says. "As George Eliot wrote, 'Ignorance gives one a large range of probabilities.' If you could read the script ahead of time, you wouldn't do anything. We'd still be in caves."

Alan summarizes his *HBR* tenure thusly: "I was leaving, having been defeated by the last part of the experience. It wasn't the place I had wanted it to be. I couldn't sustain it as the place I wanted it to be. But at least I thought I had done my duty to the place that I was personally most attached to. Now it was simply, let's see what happens."

I have not lost my mind;
it's backed up on disk somewhere.
—ANONYMOUS

When you leave a brand name like Harvard, doors that once opened easily are largely deaf to your repeated knocking. Some begin to redefine you. You do some soul-searching, some second-guessing.

The day after Alan left, "the screen went blank," as he puts it. "All those calls for speeches suddenly stopped. Was I a different person? Did I suddenly know less? Had I become less interesting? Were my ideas less valuable, my skills no longer with merit? Obviously not."

Alan Webber decided he wasn't going to let the sudden sea change get to him.

"We live in a world where brands are powerful and where credentials are still important," reflects Alan. "So if you've got a brand, use it. But don't do something just to have a brand. And don't let the brand blind you to what's important about yourself, what you want to do, or the motives of other people. People were calling me because they wanted to get an article into *HBR*. Those days were over.

"The real danger is that you become a captive of that mind-set," he observes. "You think you are the brand name, that you have authority from the brand name. So if you give up the brand name, you suddenly feel you have no authority anymore. That's a pretty stupid way to feel about yourself— that you gave away your identity to a school or to a corporation or to an administration. How lame is that? Don't think about what you left back there. Instead, think of the experiences and growth now grafted onto your life."

As to the people who confuse you with your brand name, "they don't stand up to my test of what's important," Alan says without hesitation.

**Courage is not the absence of fear,
but rather the judgment that something else
is more important than fear.**
—AMBROSE REDMOON

Alan instantly experienced an immense sense of liberation, the feeling of being entirely on his own. Leaving the prestigious safety of Harvard also meant that "the wall came down, and I started meeting a whole different cast of characters. They thought I would be snobby; I thought they would be flaky. Happily, we were both wrong. I was free to make a whole new group of friends."

That, too, was liberating.

So much of the world that previously was invisible to Alan now came into view. Alan and Bill learned from these "flaky, undeserving, weird, not relevant, without credentials people"—people who, in Alan's words, "didn't have to lie to each other to have a party."

Besides, there were other important things to do—like start a magazine, take another risk, get back the sense of excitement, the invigorating thrill of taking a chance, of going out to embrace your possibilities.

A lot of those "flakes" helped launch the 1993 prototype of *Fast Company* that became a vehicle for seeking funding. The premiere issue of the magazine came out in 1995. Then, after securing additional funding, *Fast Company* began bimonthly publication with its April/May 1996 issue. Appropriately enough, the following quote appeared on the cover: "Everything I thought I knew about leadership is wrong."

All work that is worth anything is done in faith.
—ALBERT SCHWEITZER

Fast Company has lived up to its name; it represents an unusually rapid success story in publishing. On April 28, 1999, after only twenty-four issues, *Fast Company* won the publishing industry's top honor for general magazine excellence. It might seem like one of those stories that is too good to be true. But it isn't—it has not been without its "psychological angst," according to Alan.

"Jumping into it was no big deal," he recounts. "I always knew I could pick up some consulting and editing jobs to feed the family.

"What was tough is that we would get to a certain point and I'd wonder, Are Bill and I the only ones who believe in this thing? Have we left known reality? How long can I hold out before I have to give up on the dream?

"It might have seemed like an overnight success story for this industry, but to us there were so many emotional ups and downs, so many land mines as we continued to question if what we were doing was real. Fortunately, every time I was down, Bill would be up, and vice versa."

Alan was also concerned about taking a false step. "Someone says he'll give you the money you need if you will change these five things. Should you? It's all ultimately up to you."

One thing Alan never looked for was an escape hatch. "We got our first round of capital and put out our prototype quickly in 1993. We did a direct mail test that November with forty thousand people, and our results were off the charts. We were ready to go."

If one or two people tell you that you're an ass, you can ignore them. But if three or four people tell you you're an ass, you might think about putting on a saddle.
—YIDDISH SAYING

"But then we went through an entire year of meetings, with dozens of 'almosts,' and nothing happened," Alan remembers. "You begin to wonder, How long can I ignore these messages? You do have to think, What will I do if this thing fails? But I didn't make any plans for it."

Once they knew that others recognized the vitality of their magazine concept, the moment of truth was at hand.

"You win converts, and then some converts who will write a check," says Alan. "So you have enough checks to go out with a product. The critical question was, Do we have a critical mass of customers to go from a two-dimensional concept to a three-dimensional product?

"If you do, next you have to see if enough people value it to pay for it. And then, to become a business, you need someone to write a really big check. Finally, of course, in our business, you still need to sell ads."

On all counts, the answer to Alan's questions turned out to be a resounding "yes!"

> **If I had my life to live over, I would start barefoot earlier in the spring and stay that way later in the fall.**
> —NADINE STAIR

Fast Company went monthly in August 1998, with a subscription base of 250,000. Alan's compensation already surpassed his salary at the *Harvard Business Review.*

Fast Company covers the range of attitudes and behavior, work styles, business models, financing capabilities, and aspirations that define the new paradigm of work. It maps out the territory for a new conversation about business, about the ideas and motivations that are reinventing the world of work.

Fast Company asks: Are you making a life, not just a living? Are you making a difference in the quality of life on our planet? "Work is where people have the most opportunity to influence our world and their world," Alan says. "You want to make a difference? Go into business. Go into it with a particular mind-set. Whatever it is, make that mind-set your DNA in your organization."

If Alan has any second thoughts, it's that he didn't start *Fast Company* sooner. But he has no regrets.

Alan Webber's learning process has always taken him into situations that are interesting or exciting or personally meaningful. He has never planned a path for himself and never sought to get rich.

"If you do something just to get rich," Alan notes wisely, "and then it doesn't happen, you're a failure on a level that you can't control.

"Don't do something you don't want to do. Do what you do for the right reasons with enough cover and prudent protection to make sure that you're not exposed, and the next job will follow.

"Don't let your past success get in the way. If you risk honestly, with integrity, then even if you fail, it isn't all over. It's just an invisible step to your next job. It's just your personal path."

Alan uses a wonderful metaphor for the process of shaping a magazine, for making a living that is also a life: "You begin mining. You start following a vein of possibility until it becomes a seam of ore, and it keeps leading you deeper and deeper and maybe to the mother lode.

"It starts to become real fun once you have a license to dig and some resources to do the digging with. But when it stops being fun, it's time to move on and start exploring for a new mine."

Life shrinks or expands in proportion to one's courage.
—ANAÏS NIN

✳

Lifelines

As Robert Schuller asks, "What would you attempt to do if you knew you could not fail?" How often do you hear of people on their deathbeds who wish they had taken more risks? People who, once they realize they are going to die, wish they had lived their lives differently?

When we follow our hearts and take risks with integrity and honesty, not only do we find out that the actual risks are smaller than we perceived, but we learn that the biggest risk is often taking no risk at all.

Midwesterner Alan Webber does not appear to be your prototypical "risk taker." He rose to the prestigious position of editor of the *Harvard Business Review,* then gave it up to strike out on his own. He quickly came to grips with reality when "the screen went blank" after he severed his ties with the Harvard brand name. Unfazed by the shifts in other people's perceptions of who he was, he went back to being just Alan Webber.

For Alan, his risk taking was, in many ways, a natural progression in his career. He was confident that following his passion for making a difference, doing what he wanted to do, would open new doors into jobs well suited to his mission. It was a "natural" progression in the sense that, by doing what he cared about, he encountered people through "luck" or "chance meetings" who helped him transition into his next job as co-founder of the rapidly successful business magazine *Fast Company.*

You never realize how much you can do unless you stretch. Taking risks is essential to every leader's journey. That's how you reinvent your past success. And when it is done with integrity, there is really no risk at all.

DON'T LET SUCCESS STAND IN THE WAY OF OPPORTUNITY

Don't be afraid to follow your bliss, and doors will open where you didn't know they were going to be.
—JOSEPH CAMPBELL

CHAPTER 12

✴

HONOR THE PAST, CELEBRATE THE PRESENT, EMBRACE THE FUTURE

Leni Joyce's Renaissance

Even if our efforts of attention seem for years to be producing no result, one day a light that is in exact proportion to them will flood the soul.

—SIMONE WEIL

**If you think you're too small to make a difference,
you've never been in bed with a mosquito.**
—Anita Roddick

In my twenties I devoured the writings of Carlos Castaneda. He wrote in *Journey to Ixtlan* that "the art of a warrior is to balance the terror of being a man with the wonder of being a man." I thought about that comment a lot. It seemed to reflect my deepest concerns at the time.

In my thirties I became fascinated by Albert Einstein's philosophical writings. "I was once asked," Einstein wrote, "if I could ask God one question, what would it be. I answered that I would ask how the universe began, because once I knew that, the rest was simple mathematics. But now, on second thought, I would not ask God *how* the universe began. Rather, I would want to know *why* he started the universe. For once I knew that, then I would know the purpose of my own life."

As I entered my forties I came upon an old Hasidic story in which everyone is admonished to wear a coat with two pockets in order to receive God's messages. In one pocket the message is "You are nothing but one of millions upon millions of grains of sand in the universe." In the other pocket the message from God is "I made the universe just for you."

I had an answer, of sorts, to the question that puzzled me—the question of life and purpose.

Maybe Charles Dickens expressed life's conundrum most succinctly with his "best of times . . . worst of times" line. I

254

don't know. But what I do know after nearly fifty years of life is that, however you decide to approach the timeless questions, ultimately the answers are up to you. It's all in your attitude. With your thoughts you make your world.

Which leads me to a woman I have come to know well the past twenty years: Leni Joyce.

Every spirit builds itself a house, and beyond its house a world, and beyond its world a heaven. Know then that the world exists for you.
—RALPH WALDO EMERSON

Leni Joyce has experienced the extremes of life in her seventy years. She has lived with the terror of cancer and abandonment and with the wonder of life and relationships renewed. She has seen twenty years of work produce a business triumph. Having lived through times of despair, deep depression, and black holes from which she did not know how to escape, she has found fulfillment and peace in loving her grandchildren and producing products unrivaled in the world of fabrics and design.

All of this is why she exists—literally. Without it, she probably would not be here.

Her friends call her lucky. "Leni," they say, "you are so lucky to have such a close relationship with your children and to get to run that nice little business of yours. And you do all that fulfilling charity work, too."

Leni merely says, "Thank you." She is too much of a lady to say that luck has little to do with it. "The world doesn't want to hear about the labor pains," she quips. "It only wants to see the baby."

But maybe Leni's biggest gift to those who know her well is being not a role model of accomplishments, but a person whose attitude dominates her destiny. "You can see the glass as half-full or half-empty," she declares. "It's up to you. Life is a series of ups and downs. I try to enjoy the ups and keep my courage during the downs. I try to take the difficulties as challenges and turn them into opportunities."

Live neither in the past nor in the future,
but let each day's work absorb your entire energies,
and satisfy your wildest ambition.
—WILLIAM OSLER

Leni Joyce's style combines astute business acumen with the limitless generosity of a Jewish mother. It serves her well as chief executive officer of a booming specialty textile and home furnishings company.

Manufacturing began in her basement in 1978, but when the growing company ran out of room, Leni's, Inc., moved into a charming old printing plant with a red-brick exterior in Watertown, Massachusetts, ten miles outside of Boston. If you are familiar with the old textile mills of Lowell and Lawrence, Massachusetts, you might think of hers as a "mini-mill from my past," says Leni. Her main showroom is now located in Boston's Design Center.

Leni's highly successful little company grosses several million dollars a year making high-end custom weaves for private aircraft, celebrity homes, royal palaces, and the like. Her customer list reads like a *Who's Who* of the rich and famous in global business, politics, sports, and entertainment.

What makes these bare facts all the more impressive is the singular atmosphere of her company, a family business in the broadest, warmest sense of the term. Leni's workforce consists largely of conscientious Asian immigrants whose dreams and work ethic strongly resemble those of the Eastern Europeans who staffed the New England textile mills of Leni's childhood.

Leni's family employed many of those European immigrants and thought of them almost as relatives. Leni is famous for treating her workers the same way.

"She's a mother," says Kerry Hopkins, the chief operating officer of Leni's, Inc. "She understands working mothers, the need for flexibility. She understands that many of our Asian immigrants work two jobs. So they can come in early and leave early. She gives people a chance. She's loyal to us, and we are to her.

"Walking into our factory is a catharsis for me," Leni explains. "It connects me to so much of the best of my past and to what I want to be about as a person. I see all these good, fine people—many from Vietnam, from Cambodia—people we've helped get work, learn English, build a life in the United States. They have character, they care about family, and they care about each other. And an order or two wouldn't hurt, either!"

Everyone is necessarily the hero of his own life story.
—JOHN BARTH

In 1996 *The Wall Street Journal* profiled Leni's career. (An expanded version was published in a 1999 book, *The New Pioneers,* under the headline "Leni Joyce Goes Back to the Future of the Textile Industry.") The article suggested that her background of respect for immigrant workers and her socially responsible workplace and community programs made Leni an exemplary leader for today's textile industry. (President Clinton agreed, requesting that she represent the United States on trade missions to China.)

Leni Joyce exemplifies a life grounded in the past that seeks to build a brighter future each and every day. She has overcome such daunting personal obstacles, and achieved such wholeness in what she does and how she lives her life, as to make her the natural star of this book's final chapter. In her deeds and her words, she has shown her son how to make a life and a living.

> **It is not that I belong to the past,
> but the past that belongs to me.**
> —MARY ANTIN

Lenore Joyce Cohen was raised in the shadow of the great textile mills of Lowell. Her father, Nathan, was the steward of Suffolk Knitting, which operated a million-square-foot mill in Lowell and a second mill in Bennington, Vermont.

The size of city blocks, the mills incorporated thousands of family lives and became the equivalent of whole towns. It was understood that the mills and their communities were one, that the mills served as support systems to the families that sustained them.

Leni's grandfather Frank Cohen came over from Lithuania around the turn of the century to found the mills. Little Leni idolized Frank. Grown-up Leni admired him even more.

The president of Malden Mills, Aaron Feuerstein, told me recently that "Suffolk Knitting and the Cohens were nightly conversations at our dinner table. They were a primary competitor, surely, but our brethren, too."

> **Sometimes a person has to go back, really back—
> to have a sense, an understanding of all that's gone
> to make them—before they can go forward.**
> —PAULIE MARSHALL

Nathan Cohen was raised as a well-to-do Jewish boy who benefited from the discipline of hard work and, eventually, a

Massachusetts Institute of Technology education. He spoke straight and clear and was blessed with a razor-sharp mind, a quick wit, and an open heart for everyone he knew. Nathan's life centered around the mills, his wife, Anne, his two daughters, and his philanthropy, notably his role as a founding trustee and benefactor of Brandeis University.

Whereas Nathan was nonconfrontational, Anne Cohen was the strong one, the fighter—for herself, her husband, her family. She was a homemaker, entertainer, decorator extraordinaire. Leni has inherited some of Anne's best qualities.

Helped by his brother, Peter, Nathan built a thriving company. As the family summered at their oceanside house or on their Vermont farm, Nathan made his weekly commutes between the mills and homes. In spite of old roads and flat tires, he never missed his family times. He worked hard to support the lifestyle and to make sure that he could give a considerable portion of money to friends, relatives, and good causes.

> **Anyone can observe the Sabbath,**
> **but making it holy surely takes the rest of the week.**
> —ALICE WALKER

Always a quipster, always ready for a good joke, Nat was known for his unfailing sense of humor. He was known equally for his unimpeachable integrity. His handshake or word was as good as any contract. To this day, twenty years after his death, I still run into people who knew him and who will tell me impromptu stories of his integrity and heart in business.

In one instance he agreed over the telephone on the price per pound for a large order of wool yarn. Before the contract arrived for his signature, the price plunged 20 percent. The suppliers changed the price in the contract to the lower price. Nathan signed the contract, but only after he had changed the price back to the originally agreed-upon higher figure.

Nathan Cohen and Suffolk Knitting treated employees the same way. Several generations often worked in the family mills. Many were sons and daughters of immigrant parents who had also worked at Suffolk Knitting; others were relatives or friends. Many came from the same villages in Russia and Eastern Europe.

When the economics of the business changed in the 1960s, most mills decided to move south. The Cohens stayed. They could not conceive of leaving their community and all their friends.

And so it was written.

Most of Nathan's friends and relatives considered him soft, unable to face up to the harsh actions needed to keep the mills profitable. That's what I was told. Besides that, his strong wife did not want to move, so young family members grew up thinking that he was unwilling to stand up to her and that he refused to do what any "good" businessman would do.

Unfortunately, they did not learn the truth until after he had passed away.

The truth was that he refused to walk out on his employees. These mill towns didn't have many other businesses. If the company moved, most employees would be without jobs for many years to come.

Nathan Cohen was clear on an important point: He alone was not Suffolk Knitting; everyone who worked there was— and they were all in business together.

He was a man who acted at work as he did at home, a man who felt the business was so much more than a profit-making vehicle for the family. He never even talked about leaving New England.

In the 1970s the business went into bankruptcy.

**Love is how you stay alive, even after you are gone. . . .
Death ends a life, not a relationship.**
—MITCH ALBOM

By the Cohen family's definition, Suffolk Knitting was a success. It employed several thousand people for another fifteen years after any other ailing company would have fired them. Thousands of families remained together as one.

Nat Cohen died in 1979. Given his past wealth, he left a modest estate—a few hundred thousand dollars. But the legacy paid off handsomely.

For one thing, it enabled Leni Joyce to build her own textile business with its own homey atmosphere so reminiscent of her father's mills. She can still conjure up the smell of those mills, and she often awakens in the night hearing her father's advice, especially his last words: "Whatever you do, make it beautiful, and you will always have a market."

Just as it is taught in the Jewish holy book the Talmud, Nat Cohen's legacy did not stop there: "When you teach your son, you teach your son's son."

As his grandson, I thank you, Papa Nat.

Let me listen to me and not to them.
—GERTRUDE STEIN

As the older daughter of traditional parents, Leni grew up a stereotypical good girl with good grades and good manners—all the while masking painful shyness and scant confidence. Although she was accepted by Wellesley College, she preferred a smaller, less competitive school instead, which her mother evidently viewed as only a necessary detour on Leni's way to a proper marriage with a substantial Jewish husband.

Leni wasn't expected to work, develop her interest in science, or pursue any other passion inconsistent with her pre-destined future as her mother's clone. To this day, a part of Leni remains a closet ballerina.

Leni's intended had all the right credentials: Harvard College, Cambridge University, Virginia Law School. He was an athletic, good-looking war hero and the pride of a talented Jewish family. The match was an alliance of families.

Rarely has Mr. Right been so wrong for his arranged bride. Leni knew on her wedding day that it wasn't going to work. She had never really dated. They were not in love. But it was 1949. She had a $3,000 dress and the costarring role in a $50,000 wedding production. Her expression in the wedding pictures tells the story.

> **Flops are part of life's menu,**
> **and I'm never a girl to miss out on a course.**
> —ROSALIND RUSSELL

After their son was born in 1951, the couple moved next door to Leni's parents, and her husband began to work at Suffolk Knitting. It was a great opportunity but a situation totally devoid of breathing room. The marriage soon dissolved.

Leni gained weight, felt compelled to find a stepfather for her son, and all too quickly married one of her former husband's colleagues at Suffolk Knitting. He, too, was a disaster.

Leni tried to get some distance from her parents by moving her small family to New Jersey. Shortly thereafter she wound up taking her son with her to Florida for a quickie divorce. Giving him twelve hours' notice, she uprooted him in the middle of a school year and only five months before his Bar Mitzvah. She learned later that she had been given bad advice—she didn't have to leave the state—but she was fighting for her survival.

Leni's one love, her one joy, rejected her. Angry about the move to Florida and anxious to know his father better, her son left at age thirteen to live with his father's second family in Framingham, Massachusetts. He was delighted with his new stepmother and her three children. He had found the family Leni failed to provide.

Although she moved to nearby Weston, Massachusetts, to be close to him, their relationship for the next seventeen years was tenuous at best—even though they saw each other every Sunday and Mark's friends came over with him regularly. As she readily says today, "I cannot tell you the trauma, the pain, the darkness."

The game of life is not so much in holding a good hand as in playing a poor hand well.
—H. T. LESLIE

Leni was lost in the 1960s, fighting breast cancer and the stigma of two broken marriages. In her social circle, both cancer and divorce were taboo subjects. Her parents weren't able to give Leni much emotional support, focused as they were on helping her sister, Joan, an aspiring movie actress who was embroiled in her own marriage breakup and ill with the cancer from which she died in 1968.

Leni decided to try a job at Suffolk. There she was marginalized. She was the owner's daughter, a nice Jewish divorcée who was eager to learn, but Suffolk managers were busy dealing with southern bidders at the time, and nobody had time for Leni. "Keep busy," they told her, "but don't get in anybody's way."

She needed something to focus her life.

In her mid-forties Leni began combining her mother's skill at interior decorating and her father's nose for textiles. The small consulting business she started gradually moved upstairs from her basement to her kitchen. By 1978 she knew how to manufacture custom weaves and so summoned her nerve to take the plunge—her own company.

At age fifty, in an era when women entrepreneurs tended to be young, well-financed, highly trained MBAs, Leni was going for it. She simply didn't know any better—didn't know she was violating all sorts of rules, overwhelming odds, and alleged best practices.

"Frankly, I didn't care," she says. "I was just trying to survive. The last fourteen years since Mark left home, I had hung on, doing different things. But it wasn't enough. I was ready to grow. I needed something that expressed who I was. And, of course, I wanted to make something beautiful."

Lenore Joyce Cohen, now Leni Joyce, was fighting for her life, to say nothing of dignity and respect—especially the respect of her father and her son. But this was just the prelude to the real fight for her life eight years later.

> **Trouble is part of your life. If you don't share it,
> you don't give the person who loves you
> a chance to love you enough.**
> —DINAH SHORE

During those next eight years both of Leni's parents passed away. In 1981 Mark Albion got married and reestablished his relationship with Leni Joyce, having wasted all too many years breaking his mother's heart.

There was much happiness in the first half of the 1980s, as Mark moved nearby to begin his career as a business school professor at Harvard and Leni grew her business. But what made the waste of years even more egregious was the brevity of the reconciliation before a sudden crisis threatened to end it all.

This book begins with that crisis, telling the story of my mother's bout with advanced cancer.

Expected to live six weeks, and certainly no more than six months, Mom beat all the odds—and did it with dignity and grace. The crisis brought us closer together, with daily talks and heart-to-heart sharing about the important things in life. Thinking about it brings to mind a wonderful line from Mitch Albom's book *Tuesdays with Morrie:* "The most important thing in life is to learn how to give out love and let love come in."

> **Grace strikes us when we are in great pain**
> **and restlessness. . . . Sometimes at that moment**
> **a wave of light breaks into our darkness, and it is**
> **as though a voice were saying, "You are accepted."**
> —Paul Tillich

In March 1987, after operations and months of chemotherapy, Mom was still alive—already three months longer than her doctor had predicted. My wife, Joy, and I had visited her daily at home, encouraging her to "be an example for us."

She would be that and more.

Mom began dragging herself to work. "Just before I got sick," she says, "I'd opened up the Boston showroom—a big investment. And we had set up the first DIFFA [Design Industry Foundation's Fight Against AIDS] store next to it. I had to get into work. We needed orders, too."

Many days all she could do was just lie on the floor in her office. But at least she had made it into the office.

In March we learned of the "cure." After surgery the doctor called immediately, saying, "I have very good news. Your mom is clean." As Willa Cather wrote, "Where there is great love, there are always miracles." After a few more months of chemotherapy, we had a new life.

Sure, Mom has had some unpleasant side effects, such as loss of hearing and occasional numbness in her arms and legs. But more people are aware of another side effect: Whenever Mom's oncologist has a patient traumatized by a cancer diagnosis, he calls "Dr." Leni Joyce.

She starts with a private hospital visit. She stays in touch with her patients through their recovery. Often she lunches with them years later. As she puts it, "I serve as a visual reminder that there is wellness ahead."

> **Difficult times have helped me understand better than before how infinitely rich and beautiful life is in every way and that many things that one goes worrying about are of no importance whatsoever.**
> —ISAK DINESEN

Novelist Anne Tyler has observed that "the acts that take the most out of you are usually the ones that other people will never know about." Leni Joyce never speaks much about the hard times:

Of being the first person she ever knew to be divorced—and twice at that—in an era when young women tended to feel that a bad marriage was preferable to living alone and working for a pittance.

Of being the first person she knew to have a mastectomy in an age when those things were not mentioned, and of being single and scarred, which is how people viewed breast cancer surgery at that time.

Of surviving cancer yet again, this time leaving her "with no belly button, which my eleven-year-old granddaughter, Amanda, thinks is kind of cute . . . at least she makes me laugh about it. In fact, one day she decided to paint one on!" Leni confesses happily.

Of being hospitalized for depression at a time when people thought that word referred exclusively to an economic situation.

Of relinquishing custody of her only child for several years, their relationship chilled during seventeen long years of self-doubt and seemingly interminable darkness.

When pressed, Leni will ask, "Which story do you want to hear? Do you want the one about my happy life or the one about my tragic life?"

I'll take both.

The best thing about getting older is that you can really begin to think about your calling, your passion. . . . When I look into the future, it is so bright, it burns my eyes.
—OPRAH WINFREY

Today Leni Joyce is spiritually and physically strong. Her family life is fulfilling, and her business is an overnight success—if you can call twenty years "overnight."

Recognized as an industry figure, she has served repeatedly as the United States textile representative on official trade missions to China. And in 1996 her company began making lots of money—never her aim, but a nice affirmation from the business world. "It's a way of keeping score," says my ever-competitive mom.

For her, community involvement is the most natural of the three circles—family, business, community—in her life. Since my earliest recollections, Mom has supported medical charities with her time and resources, ranging from first-aid squads to AIDS and cancer research to Alzheimer's disease. Community service is integral to her identity.

Mom and I began to repair and strengthen our relationship in the 1980s and 1990s. We found we had much in common: our values, our interest in business, our love of family.

I admired the personal touch she brought to her business,

aptly titled "Leni's Fabrics, Made by Hand." I admired how she ran her business with the highest integrity, how hard she worked at something she loved, and how responsible she felt toward her employees. No different at work from the way she was at home. As the ancient Persians professed, "If your children look up to you, you've made a success of life's biggest job."

Leni Joyce has turned her factory into an extended family that gives everybody's work a larger meaning beyond just being a job.

Hours are flexible and geared to family needs. Employees who want to work two jobs to save up for a house or a car may come to the factory at six A.M. and be out by two P.M. and on to a second job. Looms are set up not only on the factory floor, but also in people's homes so that mothers can watch their small children as they work.

Leni Joyce doesn't hire workers. "I hire people with families, with lives outside their jobs. We just had a wedding of one of our weavers. We call her 'our hummer.' She hums all the time at work. She looked so beautiful in her gown. And, of course, she sang at the wedding!

"You cannot have it all," Leni says. "You have to decide what the priorities are. If the priorities are family and work, accommodations must be made."

The same holds true in hard times.

In the time of your life, live.
—William Saroyan

When the recession of 1992 rocked the private aircraft and home furnishings markets, Leni struggled to keep her crew at full pay. The business was bleeding red ink. The day came when the only resource left was the estate Nat had willed her. She knew what he would have done, but she wanted to speak to her son first.

"Mark, you know this is your inheritance I'm throwing into this. Who knows if it's going into anything of any worth, any merit, any value," she told him.

"I felt guilty," she recalls. "Mark's dream business had just failed. And he said, 'Mother, very few people have the opportunity to follow their dream. Don't give up. Go for it. Your life is my inheritance.'

"I never forgot that," Leni emphasizes proudly. "That kept me going."

Maybe. But it is also the dream itself that propels her, for what is passion if not the becoming of a person? "I have a very heavy sense of responsibility toward the people I work with," Leni explains. "I have a responsibility to make the money, to pay their salaries, to give them as much as I can, to create the right kind of environment."

The sense of obligation to do all of that is not only huge, it is also all hers. "With nobody else to turn to, I'm in it all by myself. I have no partners. I have no large executive staff. So when you have those responsibilities, then you know that you'd better get going in the morning."

She admits that "it's a plateful, but the responsibility itself is the motivation, the engine that gives you the energy to move forward."

**My business is not to remake myself,
but make the absolute best of what God made.**
—ROBERT BROWNING

Of course, there are rewards, Leni says—letters from clients saying "how helpful we've been, how much they loved the product, how much they like dealing with us. Those are the things that really mean so much."

Then there are the Albion grandchildren, on whom she lavishes time, attention, and endless love, and her special relationship with her son. "Being in business means that Mark and I always have a lot to talk about. We understand what the other is going through. We learn from each other.

"Make no mistake about it," Leni declares, "running a small business is time-consuming, demanding, and downright exhausting—even for someone who is not of 'a certain age.' Every day there's some trauma. Every day brings new challenges. Every day you don't know if those orders are going to keep coming in—we have dry periods, of course.

"It's like having a child. You never stop worrying about him. You're responsible for his growth, his development, well-being, survival. You have no choice. You have to get up and take care of him every day."

A business takes energy, enormous energy. "I have to push to do it," Leni admits. "I run two businesses in two locations, I try to develop family values, and I have to somehow summon the energy to do it all."

**How old would you be
if you didn't know how old you wuz?**
—SATCHEL PAIGE

For her seventieth birthday in May 1998, Mom gave me a present: the Dr. Mark Albion Scholarship for biomedical cancer research at the Worcester Foundation. Endowed in perpetuity, the scholarship will subsidize a student every summer to research cures for cancer. It was the Worcester Foundation that took care of Mom after the trauma of her cancer surgeries.

Nice present, but not necessary. She had already given me a present: she stayed around to celebrate her seventieth.

Still, in many ways it didn't surprise me. I knew that her

seemingly boundless energy includes twelve-hour workdays and extra weaving done at home on her looms over the weekend or at night. Then I found out that "on the side," Mom was working on a fabric for the last old mills left in the area, too.

"We can't lose our last few New England mills," Mom says as though it were Suffolk Knitting. So she is working with a yarn dyeing company on a new high-end textile that will blend some unusual fibers with Polartec fibers, producing a potentially high-margin product in this low-margin, cost-driven industry. No charge, of course.

**What lies behind us and what lies before us
are tiny matters compared to what lies within us.**
—RALPH WALDO EMERSON

Leni Joyce honors the admirable past of her ancestors, who certainly would be proud of her today. She has re-created their mills of old in her own image, for her own times. She celebrates every day, her presence focused on the present. While our background and circumstance may influence who we are, she has shown that it is up to you who you become.

"When you realize that your time is limited, and you don't know which day will be your last," she philosophizes, "it really frees you up to live to the fullest." Indeed, while I thought she would take it easy after her second bout with cancer, she has pushed harder than ever the past dozen years.

As for the future, she is selling off her showroom business to the manager who has been running it now for several years. It will also allow her to focus on her passion, manufacturing, which, as her fabric business continues to boom, is demanding more of her time—especially when her new Canton facility is ready.

What about retirement? "I saw what happened to my father after the mills closed and he stopped working. I have no plans whatsoever for retirement," she exclaims, adding unnecessarily, "I also don't plan on getting old." In excellent health the past twelve years, she shows no signs of disproving her contention.

She hopes one of her grandchildren will take over the business but advises, "Find something that means something to you and that makes you feel you're a better person for doing it. Then get up every day, get out there, roll up your sleeves, and do the best you can. There is no absolute wisdom."

> **The great use of life is to spend it**
> **for something that will outlast it.**
> —WILLIAM JAMES

✳

Lifelines

We are all heroes of our own life story. We are all part of a bigger story, one that will outlive us. Do you know what your bigger story is? It is often found rooted in our past, connected to our future, waiting for us to live in the present.

Leni Joyce is a woman of unusual strength and fortitude— a true survivor driven by her love for her family. Her life helps me fully value the continuity of family and the heritage that came to this country in steerage with her grandfather, my great-grandfather. She has shown me how it is possible to triumph over obstacles of life, of self, of inner demons, and of outer circumstances.

It's another American immigrant story. One more step for the human spirit.

> **Nothing worth doing is completed in our lifetime; therefore, we must be saved by hope. Nothing true or beautiful or good makes complete sense in any immediate context of history; therefore, we must be saved by faith. Nothing we do, however virtuous, can be accomplished alone; therefore, we are saved by love.**
> —REINHOLD NIEBUHR

Mark Albion is donating a portion of the proceeds from the sale of his book and the audiobook to Net Impact (formerly called Students for Responsible Business).

Net Impact helps emerging business leaders broaden their business education through conferences on progressive business practices; refine their collaborative leadership skills through its LEAD program; build their networks through local chapters; and pursue their professional goals through internships at corporations, community development organizations, and social ventures.

For more information, please call, write, or visit:

Net Impact
609 Mission Street
Suite 303
San Francisco, CA 94105

Phone: (415) 778-8366

Web site: http://www.net-impact.org

For more information about Mark Albion's newsletter, please visit http://www.makingalife.com.